TH

INTRUSIVE THOUGHTS
TOOLKIT

Quick Relief for Obsessive, Unwanted, or Disturbing Thoughts

JON HERSHFIELD, MFT • TOM CORBOY, MFT
SALLY M. WINSTON, PSYD • MARTIN N. SEIF, PHD
CATHERINE M. PITTMAN, PHD • ELIZABETH M. KARLE, MLIS
WILLIAM J. KNAUS, EDD • JENNIFER SHANNON, LMFT
DAVID A. CARBONELL, PHD • AMY JOHNSON, PHD

New Harbinger Publications, Inc.

Publisher's Note

Distributed in Canada by Raincoast Books

NEW HARBINGER PUBLICATIONS is a registered trademark of New Harbinger Publications, Inc.

Copyright © 2023 by Jon Hershfield, Tom Corboy, Sally M. Winston,
Martin N. Seif, Catherine M. Pittman,
Elizabeth M. Karle, William J. Knaus,
Jennifer Shannon, David A. Carbonell,
Amy Johnson
New Harbinger Publications, Inc.
5674 Shattuck Avenue
Oakland, CA 94609
www.newharbinger.com

Chapters 1, 3, 5, 7, 9, and 12 include content adapted from *Overcoming Unwanted Intrusive Thoughts* by Sally M. Winston and Martin N. Seif

Cover design by Amy Shoup; Acquired by Jess O'Brien; Edited by Joyce Wu

Library of Congress Cataloging-in-Publication Data on file

Printed in the United States of America

24		23		22									
10	9	8	7	6	5	4	3	2	1		First Printing

CONTENTS

Part 4: Common Thinking Traps

Part 5: Intrusive Thoughts and Anxiety

Part 6: Intrusive Thoughts and Worry

Part 7: More Tools for the Toolkit

INTRODUCTION

Intrusive thoughts can appear in your mind at any time, without warning or signal. When these thoughts are persistent, repetitive, and disturbing, they can cause a great degree of distress. If you're suffering from these kinds of thoughts, you can feel hopeless, as if your own mind has turned against you.

Even worse is the sense that the more you fight against these thoughts and try to deny them, the stronger they become. Millions of people grapple with the challenge of distressing intrusive thoughts. Some have sought help and been diagnosed with obsessive compulsive disorder (OCD), social anxiety disorder, panic disorder, or other conditions, and others have dealt quietly with this challenge on their own. Whatever your situation, if you struggle with intrusive thoughts, we want you to know that there are ways to get help and find relief.

This book is designed to help you feel better. Just like a tool kit a carpenter uses to shore up a crumbling wall, this book can help you get a sense of why intrusive thoughts are bothering you, and how to change the situation to get free from the pain and suffering they cause.

In this short book, we've compiled the easiest and most effective exercises, techniques, and practices recommended by top mental health experts for relieving intrusive thoughts. These techniques all come from evidence-based treatments, having been tested and approved in research conducted all over the world.

The skills in this book are drawn from a variety of the most effective therapeutic modalities in order to deliver immediate help when you need it. These therapeutic modalities include *mindfulness* and *cognitive behavioral therapy (CBT)*, which are known to provide the most effective relief from repetitive intrusive thoughts.

- Mindfulness means acknowledging and accepting whatever is happening in the present moment exactly as it is. As a skill, it means developing the ability to notice what your mind is doing with the information it receives from the brain. This involves noticing individual acts of the mind, as well as patterns and tendencies of the mind.

- Cognitive behavioral therapy (CBT) is a type of therapy that is effective for curbing both needless fears and anxieties. The idea is that your cognitions (thoughts, mental images, memories), emotions, and behaviors blend together. Changes in one of these areas affect the others.

This book will give you skills based in mindfulness, CBT, and other evidence-based therapies to reclaim your life from intrusive thoughts. By practicing these exercises over time, you'll grow in your ability to dissolve intrusive thoughts and find peace of mind.

How to Use This Book

The Intrusive Thoughts Toolkit begins by exploring the thoughts that arise and why they happen. You'll discover how your intrusive thoughts work and how to stop fighting them. As you learn to become comfortable with the uncomfortable, you'll also explore the traps and triggers that lead to this cascade of unwanted thoughts. Once you understand your intrusive thoughts and have skills to accept them, you'll begin to examine their relationship to anxiety and worry. Then, you'll continue to build your toolkit and work on exercises that can help you soothe the distress, reduce it, and live a life freer from invasive thoughts.

This book is also designed to give you what you need when you need it, so there's no need to try all the techniques! If you find some that work well for you, stick with them. The techniques in this book can be used in a moment's notice—as needed and on demand. However, if something doesn't feel like it's working for you, drop it and move on to something else. In this book, you are the priority.

About the Brain

Before you set out to build your toolkit, it can be helpful to have some information about how your brain works and how anxiety is created.

The main sources of anxiety in the brain are two neural pathways that can initiate an anxiety response: the cortex and the amygdala. Let's take a look at each.

The *cortex* is the pathway of sensations, thoughts, logic, imagination, intuition, conscious memory, and planning. Anxiety treatment typically targets this pathway, probably because it's a more conscious pathway, meaning that we tend to be more aware of what's happening in this pathway and have more access to what this part of the brain is remembering and focusing on. If you find that your thoughts keep turning to ideas or images that increase your anxiety, or that you obsess over doubts, become preoccupied with worries, or get stuck in trying to think of solutions to problems, you're probably experiencing cortex-based anxiety.

The *amygdala* pathway, on the other hand, can create the powerful physical effects that anxiety has on the body. The amygdala's numerous connections to other parts of the brain allow it to mobilize a variety of bodily reactions very quickly. In less than a tenth of a second, the amygdala can provide a surge of adrenaline, increase blood pressure and heart rate, create muscle tension, and more. The amygdala pathway doesn't produce thoughts that you're aware of, and it operates more quickly than the cortex can. Therefore, it creates many aspects of an anxiety response without your conscious knowledge or control. If you feel like your anxiety has no apparent cause and doesn't make logical sense, you're usually experiencing the effects of anxiety arising from the amygdala pathway. Your awareness of the amygdala is likely to be based on your experience of its effects on you—namely bodily changes, nervousness, wanting to avoid a certain situation, or having aggressive impulses.

Now that you have an understanding of the brain and how it creates anxiety, let's begin to build your toolkit!

PART 1

WHAT ARE INTRUSIVE THOUGHTS?

1: UNDERSTANDING INTRUSIVE THOUGHTS

What to Know

Just about everyone has intrusive thoughts. They are uninvited thoughts that jump into the mind and do not seem to be part of the ongoing flow of intentional thinking. Intrusive thoughts are common, but for most people they are quickly forgotten and create minimal or no discomfort. For someone who isn't struggling with or worrying about intrusive thoughts, they provide weird, uncomfortable, or even funny moments… and then they are over. Sometimes they startle. Most intrusive thoughts—no matter how bizarre or repugnant—occupy only a few moments. People rarely mention them or think about them again. They're just not worth mentioning (unless they are really funny).

There are times when anyone can be reminded of a previous intrusive thought and shake their head, *Oh I remember that this is the elevator where I had that utterly weird experience of thinking that I was going to suddenly shout out an obscenity.* Sometimes—for a while—elevators and thoughts about shouting out obscenities get temporarily stuck to each other. One is associated with the other. It means nothing. The human mind just makes associations like that automatically. The experience, while strange, is unimportant and goes away.

An unwanted intrusive thought starts as just an ordinary intrusive thought, weird, funny, or repugnant as it may be. But not wanting the thought, worrying about it, or fighting with it stops it from passing quickly. Chances are, you don't want it because you're upset or turned off by the content.

But that is just the beginning. Because you worry about it, reject it, and try to push it out of your mind, it pushes back and becomes a recurring thought or image.

After a while, it starts to redirect your attention: It starts arriving with a "whoosh," and feels awful, disgusting, or dreaded. It contains an urgent feeling of needing to get rid of it. The content of many unwanted intrusive thoughts is aggressive, sexual, taboo, anxiety-provoking, or self-derogatory.

Your efforts to deal with it become all-encompassing and take up so much time, mental energy, and focus that your quality of life is degraded.

Unwanted intrusive thoughts tend to recur repeatedly and seem to increase in intensity over time. Eventually, along with an increase in the frequency and intensity of the thoughts themselves, you might start to doubt and fear your own intentions, morality, self-control, and sanity.

What to Do

Accept and allow the thoughts in your mind. Do not try to push them away. This is a complicated suggestion, but for the present, your job is *not* to distract, *not* to engage, and *not* to reason away.

Don't allow yourself to start exploring the ideas or content of your thoughts. Don't try to come up with a plan or solve any problem that appears to be created by your thought. When you do this, you're trying to figure out the answer to a problem that has no answer. Furthermore, it is not a problem!

Accept and allow means that you're *actively* allowing the thoughts to be there, not wishing they were gone, because this attitude helps you grasp that the thoughts are unimportant. They do not require any attention or response. You might even welcome the thoughts as another opportunity to teach the brain a different way.

2: YOU ARE NOT ALONE

What to Know

We have minds that worry and predict and define and create. There are infinite possibilities for what any particular mind does in any particular moment. The output of a mind could be anything, and it's always tainted by memory and fear and habit and conditioning and a gazillion other factors.

We live in the creative process of life, not only in the momentary creation. The fact that we think is far more universal and more grounding than what we happen to be thinking in any given moment. The fact that we're always feeling is far more significant than what we happen to be feeling in any given moment.

All minds produce specific thoughts. The what—the worries, fantasies, predictions, preferences, hopes, dreams, memories, fears— make up our very human experience of life. They aren't to be discounted or dismissed.

But can you see how caught up in the what we tend to get and how much suffering that causes? When we're losing sleep over what might happen, or when we're trying to out-think our intrusive thoughts, or when we walk around feeling as if we've been depressed for decades and change is hopeless, all we see is the output—the content of our experience that feels like a rock-solid statement about who we are and how our life is.

What to Do

Say this aloud: "I don't know."

It feels good, doesn't it?

There is enormous freedom in remembering how little we actually know. Our mind talks nonstop about everything it thinks it knows. It fills in the blanks of what it doesn't know to sound like it does know. It's a big ole' know-it-all.

It does this because it loves us, because it equates knowing with our security and survival. But our mind's reasons and conclusions are often inaccurate. Our mind's theories, often formed in moments of insecurity, consist of made-up rules about how we need to be in order to survive.

3: THOUGHTS THAT GET STUCK

What to Know

The thoughts you most do not want to have are the ones that get stuck. Of course! That makes so much sense. So, we find that people who are struggling with violent thoughts are people who value gentleness, find violence abhorrent, and live nonviolent, caring lives. People who have felt assaulted by thoughts of hurting others are loving people. That is why these thoughts are fought—and then become stuck. Similarly, people who believe that all vulnerable people and living things should be protected are people who fight common intrusive thoughts that sometimes involve actions like abusing children, throwing cats out windows, and dropping babies.

These are the thoughts you fight—and because you fight them, they stick. If you're someone with strong religious beliefs, you sometimes come up with blasphemous and worrisome thoughts about not being faithful. These are the thoughts you fight...and they stick. Thoughts about chairs and fruit salad and trees don't stick because they are neutral thoughts. Neutral thoughts are not fought because no one cares about them—so they don't stick.

So, the content of unwanted intrusive thoughts is the *opposite* of what you want to be thinking about. It is the opposite of your values, the opposite of your wishes, and the opposite of your character. It is the opposite of you. Unwanted intrusive thoughts get stuck because you inadvertently fuel them by trying to push them away.

As we've shown in chapter 1, the thought and the resultant whoosh of distress are automatic, which is what we call the *first fear*. This lies outside of your control. But sometimes first fear doesn't go away quickly. In fact, sometimes first fear is just the fuse that sets off a whole series of fearful reactions. When that happens, this *second fear* sets the stage for unwanted intrusive thoughts to occur. Specifically, let's say that you react with a whoosh of first fear to the intrusive thought, *I could jump off this balcony.* Then you may think, *What if I actually do it?* or *How can I be certain that I won't?* or *Does this mean I am suicidal without realizing it?* or even *Whatever is wrong with me must be serious.* These are the inner voices that keep the fear going.

What to Do

Say lightly to yourself, *These thoughts are automatic and are best left alone.* Simply stating these facts gently to yourself helps to disentangle yourself from your thoughts. Thoughts are just thoughts. Junk thoughts are still junk thoughts. No need to do anything. Remind yourself to differentiate between what you can and cannot control.

Leaving the thought alone allows your natural calming process to take over and helps you avoid entanglement. Anything you do at this point that involves effort tends to push first fear into second fear. This is the point where, paradoxically, effort to get rid of the unwanted thought actually prolongs it and makes it seem more dangerous. Leaving the thought alone may feel like the opposite reaction, but it's the best way to release the grip on the thought. Think of the Chinese finger trap, in which you have to do the opposite of your common-sense reaction to free yourself. Or think of having a tug-of-war with thoughts and what happens if you just drop the rope.

Your job is to remind yourself of what you already know. Intrusions, whooshes of fear, and the tendency to label the thought as dangerous all occur very quickly. But you're working to remember at that moment to call up what we refer to as your Wise Mind and say, *I can sit this one out.*

4: THOUGHTS ARE THOUGHTS, NOT THREATS

What to Know

The primary difference between people with obsessive compulsive disorder (OCD) and those without it is not the content of the thoughts, but their perspective on the thoughts. If your perspective is that a particular thought is "bad" in and of itself, then that thought may become problematic.

A number of factors can influence how a thought becomes "bad." When you're totally relaxed, a thought about snapping and doing something crazy may seem unworthy of attention, like junk mail. When you're anxious, that same thought may seem like a terrible indictment or warning of a nightmare to come: *If this is in my head, I have to get it out!*

If you can imagine your thoughts as a line of train cars, people with OCD and related disorders tend to keep stopping the train to make sure everyone has a ticket. Instead, simply observe the train as it passes. You're only at the station on your way to work. You don't have to involve yourself in ticketing and making sure the right people are on the right trains. This means acknowledging that unwanted thoughts are occurring, but not evaluating those thoughts as being particularly meaningful. Instead of changing what the thought means, you change your perspective toward the thought and how you process the fact that the thought occurs. It's not happening *to* you. It's simply *happening.*

Another way of considering that thoughts are thoughts, not threats, is to look at how you view words. When you see a word, you call it the thing that it relates to. In the excellent workbook *Get Out of Your Mind and Into Your Life,* Steven Hayes (2005) describes how the mind is made up of a network of "relational frames" in which concepts are experienced internally as things they relate to. When you experience an intrusive thought, you're also being made aware of all the things to which you relate that thought. For most thoughts, this doesn't trouble you, but when you have an obsession, you perceive any associated thoughts, feelings, and sensations as having greater value than they really do. It's not just the obsession, but also all things that you associate with it.

What to Do

Practice. To notice how the mind works, look at this word: MIRROR

Ask yourself, *What is this?* Well, it's a mirror. Right, it's a mirror. However, if you stared at this page and tried to do your hair or makeup using it, we would consider this a bit odd. You don't see your reflection in the preceding mirror. So, it's not a mirror. It's the word "mirror." But is it the word "mirror"? Yes and no. We call it a word, but "M-I-R-R-O-R" is really a string of letters in a specific order that makes us think of a word that we relate to a reflective glass surface, called a "mirror." In a different order, it would just be a bunch of letters. "MRRIOR" doesn't mean much. And what are letters anyway? Just symbols, little drawings to which we've agreed to assign a certain value. This is an "M," this is an "R," and so forth. So, a series of meaningless symbols is given meaning and then put in an order that adds to its meaning. This series of symbols is now called a "word," and this word triggers an idea. This idea triggers images—in this case, of a reflective surface—and all related thoughts, feelings, and sensations that accompany an awareness of being near a reflective surface.

You may experience an unwanted thought as if you opened this book and an actual mirror fell out onto the floor. The thoughts are presented as having intrinsic value, automatic importance, and urgent relevance to some behavioral response. Mindfulness practice suggests that you view the thought in much the same way as you look at words. They are empty vessels that are given power after the mind organizes and considers them. The thought of being contaminated isn't the same as being contaminated. It's a thought of it.

5: INTRUSIVE THOUGHTS ARE NORMAL

What to Know

The fact is that *everyone* has passing weird, aggressive, or crazy thoughts. If every thought spoke to our underlying character, then 90 percent of people would be weird, aggressive, or crazy. That is because about 90 percent of people acknowledge having intrusive thoughts that they characterize as weird, aggressive, frightening, or crazy. And think about some of the horror movies and TV shows that are so popular these days. Perhaps you're unable to watch them because they trigger too much fear. But remember that these awful, weird, aggressive, and crazy scenarios are thought up by normal, creative people. They are simply writing scripts that other people will want to watch.

It's a myth that weird or nonsensical thoughts indicate loss of control over your mind or even mental illness. It's also false that if you have repugnant intrusive thoughts, it could mean that you're a perverted or disgusting person.

People with unwanted aggressive or violent thoughts may become fearful that they are violent or angry *despite having no awareness of these emotions,* and that their true feelings are indicated by these thoughts. Not only may they come to believe that they must be bad people at their core, but they may also feel an extra burden to exercise serious control over these thoughts.

The truth is we all have mental activity going on outside of awareness, and it's interesting to wonder how certain mental events happen to pop up. But there is no truth to the idea that blips of intrusive thoughts and images reveal underlying truths. It is not true that intrusive thoughts reveal motives, feelings, and intentions that are deeply meaningful or contain messages that need to be addressed *when they differ from conscious thoughts, feeling, and intentions.*

What to Do

Allow time to pass. Don't urge it on. Observe your anxiety and distress from a curious, disinterested point of view. Do not keep checking to see if this is working; just let the thoughts be there. They are thoughts. There is no hurry. Allowing time to pass is one of the most important skills for recovery. Remember that any thought that produces a repeated feeling of urgency is a sign of anxiety. A feeling of urgency is discomfort, not danger. It comes automatically with the thoughts, but it is not a signal for action.

Slow down. Let it be. You are dealing with discomfort, not danger. Time allows your normal calming reaction to take effect, on its own, naturally.

PART 2

STOP FIGHTING

6: THE BROKEN DAM

What to Know

Imagine your mind as a village. Picture a valley floor with little huts, people, livestock, roads, and lots of streams of water, like veins connecting one area of the village to another. It's a pretty happy place but complicated, requiring a lot of attention and cooperation among its villagers.

The valley is surrounded by steep mountains and, on one side, a huge dam, larger than the imagination. On the other side of this dam is the largest body of water in the universe. It contains all thoughts that are possible to have—all thoughts. *What's the weather like in Santa Monica today? There are 31,622,400 seconds in a leap year.* All thoughts that anyone who has ever had a thought could ever have are there—including the thoughts you like, the thoughts you don't care about, *and* the thoughts you hate.

Now, because the village (your mind) needs water (thoughts) in order to function, there are many carefully placed holes in the dam that allow for a steady stream of desirable input. This water lands safely on the village floor and goes through all of the necessary streams and aqueducts for the village to thrive. For the most part, the dam holds everything back. It separates you from your thoughts. Your mind couldn't handle being aware of all thoughts at all times. Most of what goes on in the mind is a complete mystery. All you really need are some basics, just a consistent trickle of certain thoughts so that you can tie your shoes and brush your teeth.

But you may have some cracks in the dam such that extra water comes leaking through. The barrier that separates your *wanted* thoughts from the rest of your thoughts seems to be doing a subpar job.

It's not a *bad* job. Otherwise, your mind would be "flooded" all day. But it's not as effective as it could be.

You can view this unwanted stream of thought as the definition of an obsession. It's intrusive, it's undesired, and you perceive it as problematic. Your first response to it may be to climb the dam and plug the cracks with something. But this never works. At first, doing so may appear to slow the leak, but soon the crack gets bigger and the stream of obsessive thoughts gets more intense.

What to Do

Mindfulness isn't about stopping the flow of unwanted thoughts. It's about seeing the dam. It means taking a moment to notice that, although most things are working as you expected, there *are* in fact some cracks in the dam and there *are* in fact some intruding streams of thought. This leaves you with two options: pound your fists against the dam, hoping this stops the leak, or accept the leak as simply something that *is*. Maybe you can use the extra water to better irrigate the crops of your mind. Or maybe this water has no specific use and you need to learn to live in a wetter climate. In the end, there's only acceptance. Let the thoughts in. Let them mingle with the other thoughts. Let them simply *be*, and accommodate them by changing your perspective on the value of their presence.

Framing the presence of unwanted thoughts as just the added flow from a larger body of water takes away the importance of identifying them as *good* or *bad*. It creates space for you to view the thoughts as mere thoughts, without judgment and without your having to *do* anything about them.

7: THOUGHTS JUST HAPPEN

What to Know

Many people falsely believe that our thoughts are under our conscious control, and so we should be able to control our thoughts.

Fact: Many of our thoughts—and some researchers believe that *most* of our thoughts—are not under conscious control.

There are times when we welcome this fact. An insight or an inspiration can help solve a problem. Ask a poet or songwriter how they find lyrics, and they might say it just comes to them. Sometimes a thought just pops up, like a mental tic or hiccup. Ask anyone who practices meditation. We aren't in control of it, and we aren't responsible for it. Thoughts just happen. They wander. They jump around. They don't take orders. Occasionally it hits you in the face that you can't control your thoughts. Everyone has a wandering mind when listening to boring talks. A noisy room can interrupt your train of thoughts. And when was the last time you thought about an argument at home when speaking to someone at work? How often do you tell yourself to think confident thoughts, only to be aware of self-criticism and worries creeping in?

Just because you can think some thoughts on purpose doesn't mean that you are in control of them. You can't make your thoughts go away at will. You can focus your attention on certain thoughts, but that doesn't mean you have the capacity to make them go away.

Our mind has many natural voices, and their interplay makes our mental lives interesting and colorful. We can all identify an internal critical voice that stands guard, issuing judgments and comments, most of which we would never say out loud. We also have voices that monitor feedback from others, check on our physical well-being, calculate how much time we have left to finish a task, and let us know what we're feeling when we tune in. There are many more. The voices are natural parts of our mind as we divide up the tasks of the day, make choices, and adapt to the demands of daily living.

Let's start with *Worried Voice*, the voice of frightening imaginings. Worried Voice is the voice of "what if." Worried Voice articulates the fears and doubts and misguided conclusions that predict tragedies and awful outcomes. This voice can seem irrational, ridiculous, even perverse, or downright crazy. Sometimes Worried Voice issues strange or urgent warnings. It interrupts, annoys, scares, and talks back. Worried Voice raises anxiety. Worried Voice is often the first voice to react to an intrusive thought or new sensation.

Next is *False Comfort*. False Comfort invariably follows the "what if" of Worried Voice. False Comfort is disturbed by Worry Voice's questions and tries to remove the discomfort. We call this voice False Comfort because it never achieves its goal. It often gives brief relief and the illusion of rationality. But it does not ultimately silence Worried Voice. In fact, it does the opposite. False Comfort almost always triggers yet another what-if or doubt from Worried Voice.

False Comfort is actually so disturbed and frightened by Worried Voice that it continuously tries to argue with, control, avoid, suppress, reassure, reason with, neutralize, or work around whatever Worried Voice comes up with. False Comfort tries hard but ultimately fails to lower anxiety. It often gets angry at or ashamed of Worried Voice and wishes it would just go away. It's afraid that some of the thoughts that pop up in Worried Voice indicate craziness, danger, annoyance, perversion, being out of control, or being disgusting. When unwanted intrusive thoughts happen, Worried Voice and False Comfort invariably launch into a back-and-forth argument. *This is the commentary that is part and parcel of every unwanted intrusive thought.*

Worried Voice and False Comfort both believe in the myth that control of thoughts, especially disturbing thoughts, is not only possible but necessary for mental health. They are quite wrong. Wise Mind knows better. Here is an example:

Worried Voice: I wish I could control my thoughts, especially when I get a bad thought. I think I'm sick.

False Comfort: What you need is some mental discipline. Try harder!

Worried Voice: I'm trying, but I can't seem to do it. I think I'm broken.

Wise Mind: Everyone's mind goes everywhere. It could be interesting to watch. I have no need to stop any of it. Nor do you. Thoughts are just thoughts, and they just happen.

Belief in the myth that you are in control of your thoughts leads to the common but unhelpful suggestion that you can replace negative thoughts with positive ones and that this will help you control what you think. The facts indicate that you can deliberately think positive thoughts and distract your attention temporarily from unwanted thoughts to chosen ones. But the thoughts you're trying to replace tend to persist and *usually return even more forcefully* to your attention. How many times have you tried to push a thought away, only to have it pop right back up?

What to Do

Pause and label. Say to yourself something like *Right now I'm having a thought that intrudes into my awareness. This is an intrusive thought. It has caught my attention because of how it feels.*

This is a process of observing yourself as you experience each intrusive thought. What emotions do you feel? What sensations make up the feeling that accompanies the intrusion? You're attempting to remain as mindful as possible, watching yourself from a curious and nonjudgmental viewpoint. Your goal is to be willing to allow these thoughts even when you're not expecting them and to try not to be blindsided by their appearance.

8: WHY CAN'T YOU JUST CONTROL YOUR THOUGHTS?

What to Know

One important attitude that many people hold about their thoughts is that they "ought" to be in control of them. They think they should be able to have the thoughts they want and not have the thoughts they don't want. Do you think about it this way?

People who hold this belief are often offended and irritated by the way their thoughts seem to defy them. Again and again, they review the evidence about the content of their worries and see that the feared events are not at all likely to occur. They tell themselves that there's "nothing to worry about." Then they go on about their business. Sooner or later, they find themselves having the same worrisome thoughts. Maybe they've even been watching for them! Then they get mad at themselves all over again, wondering why they keep having the same dumb thoughts, reprimanding themselves the same way you might reprimand a teenager who has once again left dirty dishes on the table instead of clearing them away.

The truth is, we don't have pinpoint control of our thoughts. And there's *always* something to worry about because we can worry about any possibility we can imagine. We don't need realistic danger to worry.

What to Do

Try this experiment: Think of an elephant for about twenty seconds, and then stop thinking of it. No more elephant. Take one minute and keep it out of mind. No long trunk, no loud trumpeting sound, no tusks, no eating peanuts, no running away from mice.

How did you do? Odds are you just spent some time with thoughts of elephants. For most people, the results will be as obvious as an elephant stomping through the jungle. And if it seems to you as though you had no thoughts of elephants during that minute, then ask yourself this question: How do you know? The only way you can try to avoid all thoughts of elephants is to think of what it is to think about elephants and watch to see if you do that while trying not to do it! You get elephants on the brain from every direction!

Anytime you deliberately try to stop thinking of something, you're likely to think more about it. Psychological research on the subject of thought suppression clearly shows that the main effect of thought suppression is a resurgence of the thoughts you're trying to forget.

It's the same with our emotions. We don't control our thoughts or our emotions—or our physical sensations, for that matter. The more we try, the more we get thoughts and feelings we don't want.

Your lack of direct control over thoughts and emotions may come to your attention quite clearly when some well-meaning friend tries to help you by saying, "Don't think about it," or, "Calm down!" It's probably painfully obvious to you what's wrong with that suggestion. It might even make you angry that this person "doesn't get it." And yet, you may be continually trying to use this strategy without noticing that you're using the same unhelpful method that doesn't work, and then getting disappointed and frustrated when it fails again. If it doesn't work when a friend urges you to "calm down," it's probably not going to work when you urge it upon yourself!

9: TURN OFF THE ALARM IN YOUR AMYGDALA

What to Know

To understand how unwanted intrusive thoughts work, we start with the alarm response that is built into everyone's brain. This response is sometimes called the stress response, the fight-or-flight response, or—most accurately—the fight, flight, or freeze response.

The alarm response is centered in the amygdala, which consists of two walnut-sized structures in your brain. The amygdala can be either on or off: either it triggers the alarm response or it doesn't. The alarm response is wordless—think of it like a clanging danger-warning bell. There are no partial responses or other subtleties. It sets up your body to go through a whole series of responses—all of which are helpful when you're in danger. These responses include release of adrenaline, increased heart rate, changes in breathing, hypervigilance to possible danger, tunnel vision, and a host of other perceptual changes. You feel this as a whoosh of fear or terror.

Because it is designed to alert you to danger, your amygdala is triggered by just the *merest hint* of a *possible* danger. Its job is to protect you—not to keep you comfortable—so it would rather set off a thousand false alarms and create a thousand whooshes of fear when there's no problem at all than miss one that is real. It was originally designed for primitive survival. Clanging the alarm when there's no danger is called a *false positive*. Remaining silent when there is a real danger is a *false negative*. Your amygdala sends out many, many false positive responses because it never wants to risk a false negative.

What to Do

Float above the fray and allow the feelings to just stay there. Return to the present whenever you notice you're out front in an imagined future. Move from all that thinking into your current senses. (What can you see, hear, smell, and touch?) Concentrate on *what is* as opposed to *"what if."* Surrender the struggle.

Floating is an attitude of nonactive, nonurgent, noneffortful observation. It is nondistressed, uninvolved, and passive. It is nonjudgmental. It is allowing thoughts to be there for as long as they happen to be. *It is the opposite of entanglement.*

Floating above the fray is a way to remove yourself from the turbulent experience. It is not about struggling with the thoughts. You'll eventually observe your discomfort from a curious point of view, as opposed to immediately labeling it as dangerous or unendurable.

10: CULTIVATE ACCEPTANCE

What to Know

Acceptance means using mindful awareness to shift your perspective and let go of resisting the presence of unwanted thoughts, feelings, and sensations.

The mindfulness approach comes down to one global rule: to fully accept that the thoughts going through your head are indeed the thoughts that are going through your head. It means dropping any denial that what you are thinking is anything other than what you are thinking.

You may find that you struggle with the word "accept" when you apply it to your intrusive thoughts. Although the thoughts cause you great pain, accepting them means accepting that they are a part of you, that they *could* mean something. We don't want to accept them. We want them to go away! But by accepting our thoughts as thoughts, feelings as feelings, and so on, we actually allow them to go *through* us rather than get stuck inside us.

When you resist a feeling, like anxiety or fear, you don't destroy that feeling. You simply push it aside. Every time you experience discomfort and push that experience aside, you stack it on top of the last one. So, every time you're triggered, you deal with not only the experience you're having, but also the large stack of pain you've been building up.

What to Do

Try choosing acceptance as your first response to take some of that pain off the stack and start dealing with challenging experiences as they are in the moment. This is the first step in practicing mindfulness.

Acceptance doesn't mean defeat, and it doesn't mean that what you accept is the *meaning* behind *the content of your thoughts*. What you're accepting is merely that those are the thoughts that your mind receives from your brain. So, when faced with intrusive thoughts, always start with acceptance, and return to acceptance immediately after any other techniques you might use.

To fully accept a thought, you have to be willing to accept that the thought *may* have meaning.

This doesn't *give* the thought meaning. To the contrary, this liberates you from having to be certain. So, when presented with an intrusive thought, start by using mindfulness to take an observational, nonjudgmental stance toward what's happening. *I'm having a thought about being contaminated* is a much different experience from *I'm contaminated, and I'll die if I don't wash right away!*

Acceptance is not an action, but the absence of action. It can be immensely frustrating to grapple with "How can I accept that?" Instead of focusing on how to make acceptance happen, take a mindful look at the ways in which you're resisting. Find those areas of resistance; the *action* you seek is letting go of those.

Some Buddhist traditions liken acceptance of intrusive thoughts to a bird taking flight. For the bird to fly, it must have two wings: mindfulness (or the wisdom of seeing clearly) and self-compassion (or being consistently nonjudgmental and loving toward oneself).

In overcoming your intrusive thoughts through acceptance, both of these are required. Rather than run around in a circle with one wing, taking flight must include acceptance of your intrusive thoughts as just thoughts, and unconditional positive regard for yourself as you make this shift.

11: ACCOMMODATE YOUR INTRUSIVE THOUGHTS

What to Know

Our inner struggles frequently involve conflicts between our negative and positive self-views. We have conflicts between anxiety and self-mastery, doubts and self-command, certainty and uncertainty. Through *accommodation thinking*, you can see which has the greater validity.

Accommodation means adjusting to new ways of thinking and acting. Suppose you think poorly of yourself and feel anxious because you believe that others think as badly of you as you do of yourself. Yet you routinely receive positive feedback from others. How do you reconcile this difference? How do you resolve this disparity between what you think of yourself and what others are telling you? If you cling to negative information that you believe about yourself, then you're resolving uncertainty by confirming a negative self-view. If you take positive feedback into account, then you're accommodating to positive feedback about yourself.

Examining disparities between anxiety beliefs and observations that contradict those beliefs can prompt conflict, and conflict correlates with an unpleasant feeling of tension. But how bad is the feeling of tension? Can you accommodate it?

What to Do

To create a more accommodating attitude, you can redirect your thinking toward the benefits of solving fear-related problems and reducing uncertainties. A short- and long-term benefits analysis is a classic way to gain perspective on this issue. First, it's important to understand the cycle of anxiety. This refers to the fact that as a result of anxiety, you avoid your fears, which serves to heighten your anxiety, leading to further avoidance, and so on. In this exercise, you compare the short-term benefits of repeating anxiety cycles with the long-term benefits of living through the discomfort of working through your anxieties and fears.

For you, accommodation might mean reconciling conflicting thoughts about an intolerance toward uncertainty and the reality that life is filled with ambiguities. By placing yourself in conditions of uncertainty, you can come to know the problem better, and this awareness can reduce uncertainty. You'll often find that what you feared wasn't as bad as you expected it to be. If what you hope to happen doesn't pan out, you can make adjustments in your thinking and actions.

Your anxiety may increase when you think seriously about what might happen as you start to address your anxieties and fears. True, there are many uncertainties. You may not be sure of where to begin. You could feel awkward and self-conscious as you start to experiment. You may believe that you're helpless to change your anxieties about uncertainties.

Perhaps part of the answer lies in recognizing that you have evidence that you can make voluntary changes. You can change unwanted parts of your thoughts, feelings, and actions, even if changing is difficult and you have no guarantees. But this is where you want to be—at the precipice of clarity.

PART 3

BECOMING COMFORTABLE WITH DISCOMFORT

12: GET DISCOMFORTABLE

What to Know

Why should you make yourself more uncomfortable on purpose? Aren't you reading this book in the hopes of becoming *less* uncomfortable?

The answer is that we want you to do better than just feel more comfortable. Our ultimate goal is to help you end your suffering. That means taking a larger perspective and agreeing to put up with more discomfort in the present so you can suffer less in the future. The way to the other side of troubled water is through it since there's no effective way to run around it. And we know that to rewire the brain—which research shows we can do—we have to activate fears to change them. The good news is that practicing isn't as frightening as you might imagine.

Remember that your amygdala is just an alarm system. Think of it like an infant—it has no subtlety or words—so you can't teach it new information by using words. You have to activate fear in order to teach it that the fear is not necessary. When you actively and willingly trigger the fear pathway, you allow your brain to be rewired. That allows fear to decrease, and your brain to adopt an attitude of acceptance.

By now you've learned a great deal about how your brain and your body create and continue to power your unwanted intrusive thoughts. *Exposure*, a technique involving intentionally encountering a fear, gives you the opportunity to put in effect the information you've already learned. Exposure is the way to turn your learning from "knowing in your head" to "knowing in your heart, brain, and body." Exposure is the opportunity to train your brain to change.

What to Do

Think the thought—the worst thought—but with a twist. Since the thought frightens or disgusts you, one of the best ways to practice exposure is to invite the thought to enter your awareness in a slightly altered way. Stay connected to the thought while accepting and allowing the feeling to remain. Here are some ways that you can practice having your most uncomfortable thoughts with a bit of change. And remember, humor is your best ally during practice.

- Sing the thought to the tune of "Happy Birthday" or "Twinkle, Twinkle, Little Star."

- Write the thought over and over.

- Make a poem of the thought.

- Turn the thought into a song (the Songify app is free).

- Draw or paint the thought.

- Record the thought and play it back.

- Elaborate the thought into a full script with a terrible ending. *Read it over and over.*

- Write the thought on sticky notes and paste them all over the house (the mirror, the fridge, your purse).

- Translate the thought to another language.

- Say the words backward.

- Carry the written thought around.

13: YOU DON'T DECIDE WHAT HAPPENS INSIDE

What to Know

You are not your brain. Your brain is a bodily organ, and one of the things it does is generate thoughts. You may be able to dig up thoughts, and this may make you varying degrees of clever, but you didn't generate the thoughts. You *collected* them from the soup in your brain. You have no say in what kinds of thoughts happen to occur and what kinds of thoughts your mind's radar happens to pick up. Repeatedly trying to control your thoughts, by judging them or attempting to suppress them, is a type of compulsion. You only get to decide what you *do* with your thoughts, not what thoughts you have.

The same is true of feelings. Sometimes you feel happy, and it's not because anything in particular is going your way. You just feel happy. Sometimes you feel fear that's not necessarily connected to anything important. Can we better stabilize and regulate our emotions? Sure. Can we keep our emotions from determining our behavior? Absolutely. But if all it took was simply controlling what feelings we had, we'd all be happy all the time.

Physical sensations, urges, impulses—these little bits of data we get from the body—also come and go as they please. Their relevance to your life is grounded completely in how you respond to them. Responding to them with distorted analysis or with compulsive behaviors simply highlights their presence in your life. All we have complete control over is our behavior.

What to Do

The behavioral treatment approach to mastering OCD is called exposure and response prevention (ERP), and it can be useful for managing intrusive thoughts. ERP involves purposely getting in front of your fears, either in literal, physical terms (e.g., touching something that upsets you) or in theoretical terms (e.g., imagining a feared situation), and you practice resisting the compulsive response.

ERP demonstrates for your mind what it needs to better process the false information about the things you fear. If you want to stop obsessing about something, you have to stop responding to thoughts and feelings about that thing as if they were important. To do that takes practice. You have to *expose* yourself to the things, ideas, and/or feelings you fear, and you have to *prevent yourself from having the response,* which would be the compulsion to neutralize, suppress, or otherwise undo whatever your brain presents to you.

When we choose to change our behavioral reaction to an unwanted thought, we may at first feel very uncomfortable. But eventually our minds adapt to this new pairing through a process called *habituation.* By stopping our compulsive and avoidant behaviors, we stop the negative reinforcement and learn over time that we *can* tolerate the presence of our unwanted thoughts.

The end result is that thoughts that were once a *trigger* are no longer so triggering. Essentially, by repeatedly encountering our fears without compulsions, the brain tires of sounding the alarm of fear, anxiety, or disgust just to have us ignore it! The alarm gets quieter and quieter with continued practice, so being *unimpressed* by your triggers becomes the new *habit.* As you witness this change in your brain, you learn that, without compulsions, your distress goes away simply with time.

Naturally we want to see our fears subside when we put in the hard work of gradually exposing ourselves to them, and it's extremely rewarding when they do. The model is simple: start with something a little scary and overcome it, move on to something scarier and overcome it, and so on. But there are two problems with relying on this approach exclusively. First, fears, being a natural part of the human condition, often fail to go away completely and often come back like the embers of a campfire that haven't been extinguished. You may have noticed your own thoughts and fears subside and return many times. Second, and perhaps more importantly, a focus on getting fear, anxiety, disgust, and other forms of distress to go away plays into claims that we shouldn't have these feelings and that the goal should be to flee from them when they arise. To be mindful involves having the capacity to make space for distressing experiences, neither running from them nor letting them get between us and the things we value. So, while it's good to see habituation occur—that is, it's useful to feel less distress in the presence of the same trigger—learning to stand *still* in the presence of distress and make noncompulsive choices is another important way to understand ERP.

14: FACING STUCK THOUGHT OBSESSIONS

What to Know

Obsessions come in many forms and can involve thoughts, images, or impulses. As a reminder, what distinguishes these thoughts, images, or impulses as obsessions is the fact that they are perceived as bad and that they cause anxiety and distress. "Stuck thought" obsessions have a similar nature to real event and false memory obsessions in that they emphasize a fear of having to think about something distressing forever. It could be about literally anything. For example, you may look at a painting and the number twelve enters your mind. You start to worry that whenever you look at that painting, you'll think of the number twelve. The number has nothing to do with the painting, but the more you try not to think of it, the more the thought sticks.

Another example might be becoming aware of a distressing violent or sexual thought while meditating. The thought itself is not triggering a fear of engaging in a bad act, but the distress comes from concern that the thought will stay and all of your meditation experiences moving forward will be colored by the presence of that thought, stuck in your head. Another example may be a relationship-themed obsession where the concern is never being able to stop having upsetting thoughts about your partner's past. What connects all of these examples is the resistance to one object of attention being permanently associated with another object of attention.

Compulsions are behaviors (including mental acts) we engage in to try to avoid the distress caused by obsessions. Although compulsions often provide us with temporary relief, this relief actually serves to reinforce the obsession, making it more likely that we will continue engaging in the compulsive behavior. Here are some compulsions common to stuck thought obsessions:

- Mental review, mental checking, and rumination to determine whether the real event was resolved, whether the thought is a thought intrusion or a memory, or whether the thought is still stuck

- Reassurance seeking (including self-reassurance, rationalization, and confessing) about the event, feared false memory, or stuck thought

- Avoidance of things that trigger the unwanted thoughts about the event, feared false memory, or stuck thought

- Washing or superstitious rituals aimed at eliminating the unwanted thought

- Repeating behaviors, trying to engage in tasks without the thoughts in mind

What to Do

Stuck thought, real event, and false memory obsessions can be incredibly painful. Like all obsessions, they call into question what is real and what thought content you're willing to live with. The more you try to make sense of them, the more you feel stuck with them. The more you try to understand the event from your past that you obsess over, the harder it is to believe that the event happened—however, it happened and that's that. The more you try to get certainty that a thought of having done some undesirable thing isn't a memory, the more it seems like you're just denying some dark truth. The more you try to separate a stuck thought from whatever it appears to be attached to, the stronger the glue that binds it becomes. The key to accepting when thoughts like these arise is to remember to *also* accept the feelings of frustration that come with them, the way they beg to be analyzed.

It's important to remember what we're challenging when we use cognitive approaches like this. We are not challenging the content of our thoughts and trying to get to some place of "Oh, but that's okay" or "That's not a memory" or "It'll go away in time." We're challenging the assumptions behind our thought's conclusions about the danger we're in.

You can challenge that assumption by simply acknowledging that feelings may be painful and confusing, but that doesn't mean you're required to do your compulsive analysis right now. Magnifying the significance of having a thought stuck in your head, overestimating your responsibility for making sure a scary thought is not a memory, or focusing on the idea that you should *always* resolve issues from your past are also very likely to be present with these types of obsessions.

It may be tempting to think of obsessions about real events as not being a "what if" problem, but a "that happened!" problem. But the truth is what keeps you perseverating on the event is still a what-if question: *What if* it's not possible to accept what happened? *What if* there's a detail about what happened that would change this? *What if* the event defines my identity in some way, and *what if* it's some way that I can never live with? So, mental scripts for this kind of theme can start with a brief and exclusively objective description of the event itself and then get into all of the "…and this might mean" and the "…and that could result in" commentary. False memory obsessions can start directly with, *My thought about XYZ could be a memory and…* Stuck thoughts can be scripted along similar lines, beginning with, *My thought about XYZ may forever reside in the forefront of my mind and…* To target these types of obsessions, you can rewrite the mental script you recite when unwanted thoughts arise by asking yourself, *What happened, could have happened, or might happen with my unwanted thought?*

15: FEELINGS AREN'T FACTS

What to Know

Of course, we use our emotions to make sense of reality. It's just that our intrusive thoughts are always hitting the "fear" button, so we find ourselves thinking that something must be true because it just feels that way! Your upcoming performance feels as if it will be a disaster because you're nervous. You may think you'll be violently attacked because you feel unsafe. Challenging emotional reasoning requires separating *having a feeling* from the *meaning* that the feeling may imply. Feeling at risk doesn't place you at risk. Feeling ashamed doesn't make you a person of low worth. What are ways in which you notice yourself thinking that things are true only because they *feel* that way?

What to Do

You can challenge thoughts that something bad will happen or has happened because it *feels* that way by simply stating that what you feel and what you *do* don't line up 100 percent of the time. The mindfulness element here is that you acknowledge that the feelings you have are simply the feelings you have. Your thoughts may insist that these feelings must *mean* something. You're challenging that *logic*, not whether it's right or wrong.

For example, a statement of emotional reasoning for someone with violent obsessions might be, *I'm going to hurt someone, because I feel angry and freaked out.* A challenging statement might be, *I feel angry now and don't know what's going to happen, but typically my being angry doesn't result in people getting harmed.* How can you challenge some of your mistaken assumptions about feelings as facts?

16: THANK YOUR THOUGHTS

What to Know

When dealing with anxious thoughts, Eric's instinct was to block them out. When that didn't work, he'd argue back, coming up with rationales for why there was no need to worry. And like all of us, Eric seldom had much success. Our mind is a force of nature, and like with all irrepressible forces, what we resist persists. You cannot ignore, suppress, or debate with the mind logically! To your mind, your attempts to *not* think about the perceived threat will only confirm the threat, guaranteeing more chatter. To send the mind the message you want to send it, that *I am aware of this problem and I can handle it*, you must give it full voice.

Giving the mind full voice, of course, does not mean following its lead. Simply notice the chatter without judging it or reacting to it. Notice the sound of the mind like you notice the announcement at the airport warning you not to leave your baggage unattended. No matter how troubling or repetitive a thought is, just keep noticing it, over and over again. By simply noticing, you're allowing yourself to have negative thoughts—yes, even big bad scary ones you'd be embarrassed to share with anyone—and training yourself not to treat them as a call to action.

You're creating a healthier distance between you and your mind, becoming an observer rather than a participant in the worry process.

What to Do

When your mind's chatter becomes loud enough to distract you, which it most certainly will, your practice will be to observe the anxious thought and move on. To remind yourself that you're declining to engage with your mind's chatter rather than trying to shut it up, try acknowledging these thoughts with a simple *thank you*.

That's right, be polite! Your mind, misguided as it is, is just trying to do its job of keeping you safe. Like a tantrum-throwing toddler, the mind will not be quieted with reason. Like a fire alarm, it cannot be ignored. So, acknowledge the mind politely and move forward.

Remember that it's only a thought you're observing, a thought that is the product of a hijacked brain. Every time you observe it and decline to act on it, the distance between you and that thought grows, and you regain more control of your cognitions. Each repetition of observing chatter, acknowledging chatter, and letting go of chatter will, like any exercise, make you stronger and more skillful at reclaiming your own brain.

If you find yourself countering your mind's chatter with arguments of your own, stop. The mind does not learn from reason or debate. The mind learns by either a) receiving confirmation of its perception of threat, or b) not receiving confirmation of its perception of threat. You've been teaching your mind the wrong lesson your whole life by confirming its perceptions with resistance. It's time to stop. The clearest message you can send a chattering mind is to observe it, thank it, and return—over and over again—to your new expansive strategy and mindset.

Your goal is to override the mind's call to action, not to drown it out or undermine it in any way. You're building immunity, so that no matter how loudly or how often the chatter strikes, you can continue to move purposely toward your personal goals and expand your world.

PART 4

COMMON
THINKING TRAPS

17: ALL-OR-NOTHING THINKING

What to Know

We live in a world that seems very black or white. Movies have good guys and bad guys; things are often described as clean or dirty, pure or evil, safe or dangerous, and so on. But this is not the real world.

Real life always involves some amount of gray. So, if you find yourself thinking, *I'm dirty because I touched a public doorknob,* you allow your obsessive thoughts to run the show by even suggesting that you were "clean" in the first place. You were probably somewhere in between clean and dirty, and after touching that uncomfortable public item, you were, at best, somewhat dirtier on one hand than you were before.

What to Do

If your mind is being too black or white, what would be the gray area? How could you say the objective truth that accounts for the fact that it's neither 100 percent good nor bad?

Usually discovering the gray area involves saying something more diplomatic. For example, if you were anxious during a night out, you might think, *It was difficult to enjoy myself,* instead of *The evening was ruined.* Or if you said something that hurt someone's feelings, you might think, *I'm unhappy with the choice I made to say that,* instead of *I'm a horrible person.* When you catch yourself making all-or-nothing statements to yourself, see if you can reword them to reflect the grayer reality. Don't worry about getting this right just yet. This is a skill, and like any skill, it's meant to be done poorly before it can be honed. What ideas do you have for challenging your black-and-white thoughts?

18: CATASTROPHIZING

What to Know

Catastrophizing is assuming that a feared scenario will play out in the future and you won't be able to cope with it. It sets the biggest trap of all: the idea that we can predict the future. We can't predict the future. You may be very bright and really good at guessing, but you are not psychic. Your thoughts may present themselves in such a way that you not only think about a horrible future, but also predict your inability to tolerate or cope with that future. What kind of terrifying predictions do your thoughts make?

What to Do

If your automatic thoughts start with "I will" or some other prediction, then you can always start with an admission of fact: *I can't predict the future.* Now, what could you say if you included this fact? Probably something like, *This thing may happen, but I don't know for sure. If it does, that could be bad, and I might have to come up with a way of dealing with it.* This doesn't mean that your prediction is definitely wrong. Maybe the worst thing you can think of *will* come to pass. It's okay if that last sentence spiked you a bit. It's hard to accept an idea like that. But in objective reality, you don't know if your fear will come to pass, so behaving as if you *do* know is just your thoughts working overtime. Rather than trying to convince yourself that your catastrophic fears are guaranteed not to happen, try to catch yourself making negative predictions and change your mental script to reflect an acknowledgment that the future is unknown or that you lack evidence for your prediction.

19: OVERESTIMATING RESPONSIBILITY

What to Know

Overestimating responsibility means that you feel you alone are responsible for preventing tragic events. Your thoughts may use exaggerations and twisted logic to get you to think only you could possibly keep something horrible from happening and that if you shirk this responsibility, you are evil incarnate.

Someone overestimating responsibility may excessively decontaminate things (like grocery cart handles) for the benefit of the next person who may encounter something they used. You may feel the need to move something like a coin or gum wrapper from the street because a driver might get distracted and the resulting accident would be your fault! When do you hold yourself to an impossible standard of responsibility?

What to Do

Your thoughts may say that you have to check the coffee maker at work even though someone else already did this, because if *you* don't, something horrible will happen. The thoughts say that it's important for you to be good, not irresponsible and selfish. Challenge this with something like, *Compulsively checking for the purpose of avoiding guilt isn't the same thing as being a good person. I'll have to take the risk and accept that I can't always be responsible for everything.* You can challenge the philosophy behind the idea that you must be responsible 100 percent of the time. You can also acknowledge the potential consequences of your failure to act on the thought and that you don't know for certain that they are all bad. What are some challenges to your mind's tendency to be overly responsible?

20: CHECKING AND RECHECKING

What to Know

Checking is a behavioral response to a thought, feeling, or physical sensation that involves your heightened sense of responsibility. The drive to check is a drive for certainty that something has not been left in such a state that it will cause a future catastrophe. This compulsion can be found in various obsessions, such as "just right OCD," harm OCD (involving obsessions of harming others), or moral scrupulosity, but it can also be an issue of general-responsibility fears. Checking behavior might occur in response to:

- Fear that lockable items (doors, safes, and so on) have not been truly locked

- Fear that appliances have been left on (stoves, faucets, and so on)

- Fear that parking brakes or other safety measures have not been properly secured

- Fear that correspondence (emails, texts, letters, and so on) was improperly sent or contained the wrong information

These fears send us "alert messages," which trigger checking behaviors. What are some things you feel responsible for that trigger your urges to check?

What to Do

Consider the sensation of walking around with one shoe untied, while knowing that all you have to do is bend down and tie it, but you resist simply to combat the obsessive thought.

Try responding to an alert message like *Is it locked?* with thoughts like *Okay, there are those locking thoughts I've been having. I'm breathing in and I'm breathing out, and I'm also noticing that there's this urge in me to go look again, to get certainty that I've checked the right number of times. I can feel it right here in my chest and in my forehead. Okay, I'm going to practice not minding that feeling for now. Maybe later I'll check, or maybe not. I'm going to focus my energy on this moment, breathing in and breathing out. Checking urges can hang out in the back if they want.*

21: MAGICAL OR SUPERSTITIOUS THINKING

What to Know

Magical or superstitious thinking is subscribing to the idea that thinking something makes it more likely to become an action or event, or that merely having the thought is the same as an event occurring. Magical thinking plays a significant role in the mental constructs of people with OCD, especially in regard to checking compulsions (Einstein and Menzies 2004). When you're asked to think about your intrusive thoughts and worries, you may imagine that *thinking them on purpose* would make them more likely to come true. How? Magic. You may have read disturbing things in this book and fear that they're there just for you and that now something terrible is even more likely to happen. How?

Magic. Magical thinking tricks your mind into believing things you would otherwise think are ridiculous. It does this by suggesting that your being wrong isn't worth the risk, that if your thoughts *did* have magical properties, you wouldn't be able to tolerate finding out the hard way.

What to Do

What are some ways you can challenge the magical thinking that your mind engages in? For many people, this type of thinking is easily challenged with *Magic is silly, and I don't have to be certain about these things.* But even if the fusion of thoughts and actions in your head seems unbreakable, you can still challenge the rigidity: *I don't know for certain that my thoughts will cause these bad things to happen.*

No compulsion will give me this certainty, so I'll have to take the risk if I want to get better. Assess the thought for evidence while treading carefully to resist too much analysis. For example, the thought, *My wife will get in a car accident, because I thought about a crash and didn't tell myself she's going to be okay,* can be challenged with, *I don't have any evidence that my thoughts can cause car accidents.*

22: FEAR OF CONTAMINATION

What to Know

If you suffer from a fear of contamination, then you're most certainly tired of being told that you wash your hands too much or that your showers are too long. People are quick to criticize you for all the wasted soap and water and tell you that there are people without enough to eat who have "real" things to worry about. What they don't understand, unless they also experience these fears, is that you're simply doing what you feel you have to do to survive. Letting yourself be contaminated seems like no more of an option than letting yourself be strangled or drowned. And yet, part of you knows that you ask more of yourself than others do, that everything is already contaminated anyway somehow, and that your attempts to avoid being a part of that hardly make the mere feeling of safety worth it.

When we use the term "contamination OCD," we typically refer to people who are concerned that one item that they see as unacceptably unclean will cause other things to become unclean (including themselves) and that they are responsible for making sure this does not occur.

Common compulsions found in contamination OCD include:

- Specific washing and cleaning rituals (this can be a matter of frequency, of needing to wash or clean in a specific ritualized way, or both)

- Avoidance of things viewed as contaminated, or avoidance of clean things when you feel contaminated

- Mental review of whether contact has been made with contaminants and whether washing rituals were properly executed

- Asking others for reassurance that they have not been exposed to a contaminant or have not exposed others to contaminants

- Seeking reassurance online in the form of researching your feared contaminant

- Collecting, and overfocusing on, memories of contact with contaminants

What are some of the compulsions you act on because of your contamination fears?

What to Do

Start by paying close attention to your present experience with contaminants. Imagine that you've come in contact with something that you believe is contaminated. It happens in an instant. You touched something, maybe you were just near it, or maybe you aren't certain what was touched. Immediately your thoughts, feelings, and physical sensations start presenting you with information. Your mind receives a lot of signals at once, all of them with the potential to be very upsetting if you take them seriously. First, you become very aware of the part of your body that you think is contaminated. If you focus your attention on that part of the body, you'll certainly notice that, as a function of overattention, you begin to get some sort of physical response. Your hands feel dirty to you.

What if you were able to exist with the feeling of contamination and allow yourself to see the bigger picture? The bigger picture is that no amount of washing ever gets you "clean," because your definition of the word "clean" necessarily involves experiencing a specific feeling that you call "clean." A computerized device that could measure germs wouldn't be enough. You would have to *feel* clean to be clean. Rather, to get the upper hand on the fear, practice being mindful of the feeling of contamination and all of its related sensations. Additionally, practice exposure—as we learned earlier—by allowing yourself to experience the feeling of contamination to begin to develop a less fearful response.

Eliminating a feeling by engaging in compulsions sends the message to the brain that the feeling is your enemy. Owning the feeling sends the message that it's simply an experience, like many others, and that it doesn't warrant a massive amount of attention. Consider which message will result in less perpetuation of your contamination fears.

23: EVERYTHING NEEDS TO BE JUST RIGHT

What to Know

Too often people with OCD are mocked in the media as being "clean freaks" or organization nuts. While a healthy sense of humor about the lengths we go to in order to feel okay is probably warranted, it's important to remember that for you, the opposite of feeling *just right* about something is feeling dead *wrong* about *everything*.

Just right OCD deals primarily with the obsessive fear that something is not precisely as it should be, not symmetrical, not organized correctly, or not perfect in some discomforting way. While all obsessive-compulsive behaviors are an attempt to feel "right" in some way, it's helpful to recognize this particular type of obsession and its common triggers. Typically triggers include:

- An awareness that an object or behavior is not symmetrical with another object or behavior

- A feeling of unease when completing a routine activity

- A concern that an item does not belong in a specific location

What are some things you think must be adjusted if they seem off to you?

Typical compulsions that occur in response to these triggers typically involve:

- "Fixing" objects to look "right" in a given space (e.g., straightening a picture frame or lining things up perfectly on a desk)

- Repeating a behavior that has been done on one side on the other side (e.g., tapping your right leg after noticing that you've just tapped your left leg)

- Repeating a behavior to feel "right" (e.g., repeating walking through a doorway or shutting a drawer)

- Checking to see if things appear as you feel they *should* (e.g., reviewing the placement of two pillows on a bed to make sure they are in the perfect position)

What are some compulsions you do to make an "off" feeling "just right" again?

What to Do

You may have been told, "Just move on," "Let it go," or, "Stop acting weird," receiving absolutely no sympathy for your experience. This advice is like asking someone to spend their life walking around with only one sideburn—seeing it in the mirror every day, being told it looks fine, and yet feeling absolutely certain that it must be changed.

This fear is being informed primarily by an emotional state, a feeling that something is not the way it needs to be. Sometimes this is described as an NJRE (Not Just Right Experience). Mindfulness in this situation means identifying that feeling and everything it encapsulates, including thoughts about being anxious, shame about not being able to just move on, and physical symptoms that range anywhere from basic anxiety to disgust. Once this experience is fully acknowledged, it then needs to be allowed to exist as another of life's experiences. The hardest part of acceptance with this thinking trap is knowing that the compulsion is often as simple as briefly touching something or moving something ever so slightly. It's the feeling of having relief just within reach but behaving as if it were actually out of reach. It's the image of a carrot on a stick wherein the stick is short enough for you to reach the carrot, but the carrot is there to be observed, not eaten.

Try to allow that "off" feeling to be exactly as it is. Find out where you feel it in your body: Your chest? Your shoulders? Breathe into it and carry it with you as if it belongs there. Carry it with you on your way to doing something greater than your compulsive fixing. Let the "off" feeling come along for the ride if it must, or let it fade away because you're too interested in attending to something else.

24: TUNNEL VISION

What to Know

Tunnel vision means focusing exclusively or excessively on things that relate to your fear. *Selective abstraction* is what makes you tie your every experience into whatever you're obsessed with. It's as if the things that relate to your obsession are somehow more visible. It's like hearing a lot of love songs on the radio after breaking up with someone. The love songs were there before, but you're selectively abstracting them *from* your environment and connecting them to your thoughts.

What to Do

If you notice that your mind is singling out some negative detail related to your obsession and missing the bigger picture, then take the opportunity to look at the bigger picture. What does it sound like in your mind when you only notice the obsession instead of the bigger picture? This is a true mindfulness challenge in which you can acknowledge your mind pattern: that you tend to associate things with your obsession. The association doesn't mean that these things are actually linked anywhere but in your mind. Here you can take the opportunity to respond, *I tend to notice these things because of my obsessive thoughts, but it's not necessary to pay extra attention to them just because they relate to my obsession.* How can you challenge your mind when it's zeroing in on something related to an obsession?

25: "SHOULD" STATEMENTS

What to Know

Perfection is the perpetual state in which something horrible is about to happen. Anything that changes what's perfect automatically destroys it, so perfection is an illusion—not something that we actually want, because it's not something that actually exists. Still, your thoughts throw the words "should" and "must" into the equation, and you feel helpless against them.

You may tell yourself that you *should always* be health conscious, even though you want to have a doughnut for breakfast. If you have obsessions of a sexual or violent nature, you may berate yourself for having the thoughts, believing that you *must never* think them. You may feel that you *should* be able to recall the details of *every* conversation and *must* comprehend *every* word of *every* book you read. It's exhausting. The real problem with making "should" statements is that trying to overcontrol your thoughts is mutually exclusive of accepting what *is,* and thus, destroys mindfulness. If something should be one way and it isn't, that means it cannot be accepted the way it is. That leaves no room for mindfulness. What are some rigid rules that you impose about your fears?

What to Do

If your mind says you *must* never have this thought or you *should* do this or that compulsion, challenge this by addressing the rigidity of the statement. Throw mindfulness at the thoughts: *I notice that I have an urge to do my compulsion, but there's no such thing as "should" or "must." I can choose and be flexible in my choices.* If, for example, you struggle with a compulsive urge for symmetry, you might think, *I must line up those books the right way.* Challenge this with, *I have an urge to line up those books and could challenge my thoughts by letting them be.* Sometimes it can be helpful to replace "should" with the expression "It would benefit me to…" See if your "should" statement still makes sense after that. Other than reducing your temporary anxiety, would it *benefit* you to drive back home to check whether the stove was turned off? Other than compulsively quieting the intrusive thoughts momentarily, would it *benefit* you to stay late at work, redoing a project to make certain it's perfect? What are some ideas for challenging your more perfectionist beliefs?

26: RUMINATION

What to Know

You may spend time thinking about the past and what could have been, what you did wrong, and the mistakes that you made. You think about how miserable you feel and about what's wrong with you and why you can't change. You think about what's wrong with others and why they should change. You think about what's wrong with the world and why that should change. When you feel trapped in this self-absorbing monologue, you come to know more and more about what bothers you and very little about how to escape your ruminating habit. Is it possible for you to break this cycle?

What to Do

Ruminative thinking is a core issue that commonly occurs with both anxiety and depression (Olatunji, Naragon-Gainey, and Wolitzky-Taylor 2013). If you find yourself in a rumination loop, you can use your self-observation skills to defuse this process. Here are the steps:

Step back and look at your thoughts. Nonjudgmentally *observe* (what's happening), *qualify* (what's ruminative, what's not), and *quantify* (how often, how intense, how durable) your ruminative thoughts. This examination can help to moderate rumination and worry.

Rather than look at the glass as half empty, explore what's in the other half. The world of rumination is filled with *could haves*, what you could have done or said or thought. Balance it out with memories of what you did do and are pleased with.

Reflect on the problems that you face. You can help yourself by asking productive questions and seeking verifiable answers. What are the facts in this situation? What are your options? How will you go about executing your best option? By asking and answering productive questions, you're likely to be better positioned to pursue your most promising options.

Deal with the here and now. Oscillating between regretful remembrances and anticipated dreads detracts from the present moment. Right now there is no guilt, for guilt reflects the past. Right now there is no frightful event, for anxiety is about the future. If you can't think of anything else to think about, just look at the back of your hand. What you see is what is happening right now. Not too scary, is it?

PART 5

INTRUSIVE THOUGHTS AND ANXIETY

27: IDENTIFY YOUR ANXIETY-IGNITING THOUGHTS

What to Know

Learning to recognize some common types of thoughts that activate the amygdala in a variety of situations is an important step in learning to restructure your thoughts and use mindfulness to reduce your anxiety. If you change your thoughts, you establish new patterns of responding in the brain that endure and protect you against anxiety.

Because anxiety-producing thoughts arise automatically, you may not be aware of the various ways in which the cortex—the outer layer of the brain involved in sensing, thinking, reasoning, planning, remembering, and other high-level functions—creates anxiety. In the following pages, we offer a series of exercises that will help you identify cortex-based processes that contribute to your own anxiety.

We call all of the cortex-based tendencies below *anxiety-igniting thoughts* because they have the potential to activate the amygdala. In fact, they could be a primary source of your anxiety.

One of the simplest ways to see the influence of your cortex is to consider your general outlook on yourself, the world, and the future. Part of the cortex's job is to help you interpret your experiences and make predictions about what's likely to happen in the future. Your general perspective can have a strong impact on this process. Some people tend to be optimistic and expect the best, while others are more pessimistic and expect the worst. Optimism is more common, and it tends to result in less anxiety. If you tend to be pessimistic, you're likely to be more anxious. Furthermore, a pessimistic attitude can make you less willing to try to change anxiety because you don't expect success.

What to Do

Let's look at some anxiety-igniting thoughts. This assessment will help you examine whether you tend to engage in negative, pessimistic thinking. Note that this assessment is not a professionally designed test; it's simply offered to help you consider the nature of your own thought processes. As you complete the assessment below, consider the examples carefully and be honest about whether they reflect your experience of your own anxiety.

Read through the statements below and check any that apply to you:

- *When I have an upcoming presentation or examination, I worry about it quite a bit and fear I won't do well.*

- *I generally expect that if something can go wrong, it will.*

- *I'm often convinced that my anxiety will never end.*

- *When I hear that something unexpected has happened to someone, I typically imagine it's something negative.*

- *I frequently prepare myself for negative events that I fear will occur but seldom or never do.*

- *If it weren't for bad luck, I wouldn't have any luck at all.*

- *Some people want to improve their lives, but that seems pretty hopeless to me.*

- *Most people will let you down, so it's best not to expect much.*

If you checked many of these statements, you show signs of pessimistic thinking. Read on to learn how to shift your way of thinking and decrease your anxiety.

28: CONTROL YOUR ANXIETY-IGNITING THOUGHTS

What to Know

You can change the thoughts in your cortex and shift your focus to other thoughts. This is called *cognitive restructuring*. These techniques give you the power to literally change your cortex. The key is to be skeptical of anxiety-igniting thoughts and dispute them with evidence, ignore them as if they don't exist, or replace them with new, more adaptive thoughts, also known as coping thoughts.

Pay particular attention to the anxiety-igniting thoughts you catch yourself using quite often. Your neural circuitry is strengthened by the principle of "survival of the busiest" (Schwartz and Begley 2003, 17), so the more you think certain thoughts, the stronger they become. If you interrupt anxiety-provoking thoughts and images and repeatedly replace them with new cognitions, you can literally change the circuitry of your brain.

What to Do

Coping thoughts are thoughts or statements that are likely to have positive effects on your emotional state. One way of evaluating the usefulness of thoughts is to look at the effects they have on you. In this light, you can clearly see the value of coping thoughts, which are more likely to result in calm responding and an increased ability to cope with difficult situations. Here are some examples of anxiety-igniting thoughts, each followed by a more useful coping thought:

It's no use trying. Things will never work out for me.

I'm going to try, because then there's at least a chance that I'll accomplish something.

Something's going to go wrong. I can feel it. I don't know what's going to happen.

These kinds of feelings have been wrong before.

I need to focus on this thought, doubt, or concern.

Cortex, you've spent too much time on this and need to move on.

I must be competent and excel at everything I do.

No one is perfect. I'm human and expect I'll make mistakes at times.

Of course, you'll have to be vigilant about recognizing anxiety-igniting thoughts and substituting coping thoughts, but it's worth the effort. Some people post their coping thoughts to remind themselves.

By deliberately thinking coping thoughts at every possible opportunity, you can rewire your cortex to produce coping thoughts on its own. Remember, you're changing your neural circuitry! Be sure to focus on the types of thoughts that are most problematic for you.

For example, if you tend toward perfectionism, it's useful to watch for "musts" and "shoulds" in your thinking. When you tell yourself you "must" accomplish something or that something "should" happen according to a certain plan or schedule, you're setting yourself up for stress and worry. The words "must" and "should" make it seem like a rule is being violated if your performance is less than perfect or events don't unfold as planned. If nothing else, replace "I should…" with "I'd like to…" That way, you aren't creating a rule that must be followed. Instead, you're simply expressing a goal or a desire—one that may or may not be met. It's a kinder, gentler thought.

29: STOP FEEDING INTRUSIVE THOUGHTS

What to Know

When we experience anxiety, we tend to engage in behaviors aimed at keeping us safe, such as avoidance of situations we fear or compulsions such as checking or hand washing. While we may get temporary relief from these safety strategies, our lives become constricted and controlled by our anxiety. When we replace strategies that keep us safe with strategies that help us expand, we disrupt the cycle of anxiety and make new things happen. Strategies that help us expand—*expansive strategies*—are not intended to reduce anxiety, but rather to override it.

An expansive strategy is the active ingredient in your recipe to break the cycle of anxiety. Expansive strategies enable you to have new experiences that counter your perceptions and solidify a new mindset.

And, as an added bonus, strategies that build or strengthen a cycle of expansion will teach you how to override anxiety, which will eventually lead to actually feeling less anxious. Expansive strategies are easy to come up with because they are usually the mirror opposite of safety strategies. For example, one safety strategy popular with shy people at social gatherings is to position themselves in one spot and wait for others to approach them in conversation. This strategy ensures that whomever you talk with is interested in you and thus not likely to reject you. Every time someone else takes the initiative and you are not rejected, your cycle of intrusive thoughts is maintained.

What to Do

To break that cycle, your new, expansive strategy at a social gathering might be to simply approach someone and say hello. You could follow up by asking them a question about themself, or by sharing something about yourself. Do you need to be smart and funny, the life of the party? No! That would be a bull's-eye.

By simply putting yourself out there you are right where you belong, *on the target*. Be aware that if you employ a new strategy with an old mindset—*I need to sound confident, show no signs of anxiety*, in other words be perfect—you will not make progress. You must create an expansive mindset to go with your expansive strategy. Something like, *I can sometimes be boring or sound stupid. I don't need to hit the bull's-eye; I just need to be on the target.*

Will you really believe this? Not at this point. You've been thinking with the perfectionist mindset for most, if not all, of your life. You can, however, adopt a mindset that *seems* truer, even if you do not trust it yet. The gardener who faithfully waters and weeds will see the seed sprout and grow into a lush plant. In the same way, you—as you repeat your expansive strategy—will come to believe the mindset you've been cultivating.

The beautiful thing about expansive mindsets and strategies is that they maintain cycles of expansion. Not having to hit the bull's-eye every time opens up the whole target. There's no limit to where you'll be able to go. There's a big world out there!

Of course, thinking about a bigger world is going to mean greater anxiety. If you're feeling anxious right now, good! That means you're getting it. Yes, you'll be more anxious when you drop a safety strategy and replace it with an expansive strategy. But in the short run, becoming more anxious is exactly what you need. You're standing up to your mind by saying, *I choose to be more anxious. I'm willing to be imperfect.*

When you do this over and over again, your anxiety alarms will decrease and you'll become more comfortable being yourself in social situations. You'll also learn how to deal with occasional rejection, which makes you much more resilient.

30: WELCOMING ANXIETY WITH BREATHING

What to Know

The next time you notice yourself feeling anxious, stop for a moment and pay attention to where you're experiencing the most discomfort. Is it in your chest or in your stomach? Does it make your head ache or your heart palpitate? Once you've located where that discomfort is, begin to breathe intentionally into that part of your body. Imagine greeting that discomfort with a stream of fresh healing air. This is your Welcoming Breath, a powerful way you can express your new expansive mindset.

Continue to breathe with the intention to welcome rather than resist. Each inhalation supports the space for this uncomfortable feeling to exist. With each exhale, let go of any control you may be hanging on to. Remind yourself as often as you need to: *This feeling is necessary*, and, *I can welcome it as long as it is there.*

What to Do

The Welcoming Breath will feel awkward at first. Unless we're exercising, we tend to breathe in a shallow manner with only a small portion of our lungs. But go ahead and breathe deeply, even though you aren't doing anything strenuous. You cannot hurt yourself by taking in more oxygen.

As you continue this Welcoming Breath, you'll notice that your feelings will change. They may intensify or they may decrease. They may move to a different part of your body. Other feelings may arise to accompany them. If that happens, welcome them too. Whatever happens, just keep breathing and welcoming, allowing the feelings to be there, allowing them to change, allowing them to stop, and even allowing them to start again.

To facilitate this process, open your whole body to make space for whatever needs to happen. Whether standing, sitting, or lying down, keep your back straight to allow for maximum lung expansion. You want plenty of room for the feelings to move. You may also find it useful to hold your palms open; it's another physical way of reminding yourself that you are welcoming what is happening, that you are surrendering control, that you are willing to feel what there is to feel, however it changes, moment by moment, breath by breath.

Be a relentlessly welcoming host. If you keep refocusing on your breath, you'll surprise yourself at how well you can accommodate whatever sensations or emotions arise.

Don't be discouraged if you get overwhelmed or distracted and don't see the feeling through to the end. You likely won't at first. The Welcoming Breath, like any technique, will require practice, and most sensations and feelings will arise many times before you'll begin to experience significant resilience to them, or a noticeable decrease in them. As long as you think of them as opportunities to be welcomed, you'll be growing and expanding.

Welcoming what you're accustomed to resisting will be a challenge for you. The key is to set the intention to have uncomfortable feelings. Most of us have spent our whole lives trying not to feel discomfort, so it's a big leap to actually welcome uncomfortable feelings. But that's exactly what we need to do. A necessary feeling is like an uninvited guest who always shows up anyway. Since you know it's coming, you'll be better able to handle it if you send an invitation.

31: PREVENTING ANXIETY FROM COMING BACK

What to Know

However great your progress, anxiety thinking and negative feelings may not entirely disappear. You lose a few nights of sleep, and an old maladaptive anxiety habit can creep back. However, lapses don't have to be as intense, durable, and frequent as they were before. You can recover more quickly. If you are not perfectly consistent in managing your worries and troubles, you don't have to look at yourself or the situation negatively. As the saying goes, if you fall off a horse, get back on again.

When it comes to reversals, it helps to look at the big picture. With a little perspective, you can see that you can avoid double troubles over lapsing and relapsing if you keep yourself from magnifying setbacks into catastrophes. You also can see that you have cognitive, emotional, and behavioral tools to assert control over new or older anxieties. You can see that you can tolerate tensions, which is not the same as liking them. And most importantly, you can see that life is more than just contesting anxieties. It's what you choose to make it. This big-picture thinking gives you a legitimate form of control over anxieties if they recur.

If you assume that change is a process and not an event, it's easier to accept the ups and downs of self-improvement and personal growth. Looking at change this way is far less taxing than thinking that if you slide back, everything you've done so far is worthless. Each new anxiety event gives you an opportunity to hone your cognitive, emotional-tolerance, and behavioral skills. But you don't have to wait for anxiety to spontaneously recur in order to practice. You can use these skills regularly to actualize your finest qualities.

What to Do

Deal with anxiety early! If you feel a needless anxiety stirring about something in your life, take preventative steps to stop anxiety from getting a foothold:

- Keep perspective on what is most important in your life. It can be family. It can be a passionate pursuit. Emphasize what you value over what you fear.

- Separate yourself from your anxiety symptoms. You are not an anxious person. You are a person who sometimes experiences anxiety and who wants to experience this feeling less often. By not identifying with your anxiety, you're freer to release it.

- Go on the offensive. Take the most basic step that you can take to advance against the anxiety you experience. If you have trouble motivating yourself to take this step first, remind yourself that you act against anxiety to prevent anxiety from interfering with what you value most in life.

PART 6

INTRUSIVE THOUGHTS AND WORRY

32: IT'S WORRY TIME

What to Know

Worry Time is just what it sounds like, a time for you to worry, on purpose no less! The difference is that Worry Time is *your* time. You decide when to worry and what to worry about. This makes a bigger difference than it sounds. Worry is a mental action we take in response to a perceived threat. As such it is a safety behavior, designed to forestall the negative emotions that accompany the thoughts. When you decide on your own to designate a time to allow the anxious thought to be expressed—without trying to fix or problem solve anything—you are setting the agenda. You are taking a different stance toward worry. With this new stance, you level the playing field. It's a little like standing up to a bully. The message is, *This is* my *neighborhood. Bring it on! I can handle it.*

Worry done this way, with a plan and purpose, is transformed from a safety strategy to an expansive strategy. You bring up the anxious thought yourself and don't try to resist it.

What to Do

Designate a block of time in your day that you'll devote to full-on worrying. Set your alarm or mark it on your calendar just like you would for any other important commitment. Since, as you've already guessed, it won't be something you'll be looking forward to, try planning a block of time shortly before you expect to do something fun, like meeting a friend, watching a movie, or some other form of entertainment.

When your appointment with worry arrives, find a spot where you won't be disturbed, set your timer for ten to twenty minutes, and go to it. Worry your head off. Don't stop until the timer rings. Remember not to argue against or suppress the thoughts and feelings that emerge. You are in charge and this is what you asked for. You've chosen to open the gates, letting everything you're thinking and feeling pass freely through you, resisting nothing. You'll be tempted to problem solve some of your worries, but don't go there. No fixing, just feeling!

Conversely, your mind may stray away from anxious thoughts, and you'll find yourself thinking about benign things that have no emotion attached. Refocus on an anxious thought. This is Worry Time, when your intention is to worry. The more often you return to worrying, the better!

33: HUMORING THE WORRY

What to Know

Worry is counterintuitive. When you try to remove it, by whatever means, it becomes more persistent. The point of a humoring response is to become more accepting of the worry so that it matters less to you. It's to get better at hearing and accepting the thought for what it is— simply a thought, a twitch in your internal world. It's okay to have thoughts—smart ones, dumb ones, pleasant ones, angry ones, scary ones, and so on.

We don't have that much choice in the matter. We all have lots of thoughts. And a lot of them are misleading and exaggerated. That's okay. We don't have to be guided by them, or argue with them, or disprove them, or silence them. We just have to be willing to hear them as we go on about our business.

What's a person to do? When you try to get rid of the "bad times," it often prolongs and strengthens them. When you try to hold on to the "good times," they get ripped from your hands.

Frustrating, right? Let's recall that important observation: *The harder I try, the worse it gets.* How can you apply that here? You might identify your worry thought and "keep that thought in mind." What does that mean, to keep that thought in mind? It means the opposite of what you do when you try to "keep that thought *out* of mind!" You deliberately keep the thought at hand, playing with it, repeating it, trying not to forget about it, maybe checking in with yourself every three minutes or so to make sure you remember to repeat the thought to yourself periodically. Why would anyone do that? Well, if it's true that "the harder I try, the worse it gets," you'll probably get better results doing the *opposite* of what you usually do!

What to Do

So how about doing some humoring? There are a lot of ways to do this. Here's one method. Simply take the thought, accept it, and exaggerate it. There's a training exercise in improvisational theater called "Yes, and..." In this exercise, you accept whatever the other person in the scene has just told you, and build on it by adding something else. You don't disagree, or contradict, or deny what the other player just said. You accept it and add to it. This is probably the most fundamental rule of improvisational comedy—no denial! Instead, accept whatever the other performers offer you and build on it.

This rule works on stage and will also work in your own mind, in your internal world. The reason it works so well on stage is different from the reason it works so well with worry, but this rule definitely helps with worry.

How can you use it? Here are some examples of humoring the thoughts in this way:

- What if I freak out on the airplane and they have to restrain me?

  Yes, and when the plane lands they'll probably parade me through town before taking me to the asylum, and I'll be on the nightly news for everyone to see.

- What if I get so nervous at the banquet that my hands shake so everyone can see?

  Yes, and I'll probably spill hot soup all over the bridal party and cause second degree burns, so the honeymoon will be ruined.

- What if I get a fatal illness?

  Yes, and I better call the hospital to make a reservation now, and probably the funeral home, too.

The point of this response is not to get rid of the worry. Many people are so used to trying to rid themselves of their chronic worry that they'll sometimes try the humoring response for a while, then say, "It didn't work. I still worry." That's *not* the aim of humoring. The aim is to become more accepting of your worries so they interfere less in your life. So go ahead, try a little humor!

34: REPEATING THE WORRY CAN REDUCE ITS POWER

What to Know

Your automatic thoughts are like an unending soundtrack that accompanies you your entire life. Sometimes the thoughts are relevant, sometimes not; sometimes pleasant, sometimes not; sometimes accurate, sometimes not. There's no off switch, no volume control. We live in our thoughts the same way a goldfish lives in water.

We do not get to pick our thoughts. We can, however, often pick how we respond to them, and we can certainly pick what we do with our time on this planet. We don't need to get our thoughts arranged the way we might like in order to do things we want to do. This work that people do of trying to hold onto the "good" thoughts and get rid of the "bad" thoughts—where do they do it? In their heads! As the activity of life goes on around them, they're missing out, because they're inside, trying once again to rearrange the furniture rather than coming out here into the sunlight where life actually occurs. Let your thoughts come and go in your head while you tend to the activities that are important to you out in the external world, the environment of people and objects that you live in.

What to Do

Want to try an experiment? It won't take long, although you should pick a time and place that allows you privacy, so you can focus your attention on what you're saying without a lot of concern about being overheard. You may feel foolish anyway, but please do give it a fair try. It's got three steps.

Step One. Create a twenty-five word worry sentence starting with "what if." Use a topic that you usually find quite upsetting and spend some time to get the most unpleasant ideas in the sentence that you can. State the "what if" worry and add two or three "and then" statements of the terrible consequences it will produce—include the angst you'll feel in your old age as you remember this bad event, and so on. Here are a couple of examples. (As you might expect, simply reading these examples of worry will induce discomfort in many readers. That's okay, it will pass. However, if you don't feel up to that experience right now, bookmark this section and come back some other time when you're more willing to feel that discomfort.)

Examples:

For someone who worries about losing their sanity:

WEAK: What if I go crazy?

BETTER: What if I go crazy and end up in an institution?

GOOD: What if I go crazy, end up in an institution, and live a long, miserable, pointless life—forgotten, toothless, with bad hair, abandoned, and alone?

For someone who worries about looking foolish at a party:

WEAK: What if I get really nervous at the party?

BETTER: What if I get really nervous at the party, and then start sweating and trembling?

GOOD: What if I get really nervous at the party, start sweating and trembling, pee in my pants, and people avoid me the rest of my life?

Don't just stop with your first of your "what if" statement. Take a little time to edit it and get the maximum strength—all the fear and loathing you can muster—into your wording.

Step Two. Write the numbers one to twenty-five on a slip of paper. If you prefer, you can group twenty-five small items—toothpicks, coins, jellybeans (or Tic Tacs!)—on a table.

Step Three. Sit, or stand, in front of a mirror so you can see yourself. Say the worry sentence out loud, slowly, twenty-five times. After each repetition, cross off the next number on your slip of paper or move one of the small items into a different pile, so you can keep count. Don't count in your head, because that takes too much concentration—concentrate on the twenty-five repetitions of the worrisome thought.

If you're like most people with chronic worry, you probably found that the worrisome thought *lost* power with repetition, so that the last repetition felt much less disturbing than the first one. And if you did, this offers a powerful insight into the nature of your chronic worry.

Think of all the efforts you've made to rid yourself of the worry, and how little you have to show for them. Yet here, with just a few moments of repeating your worry out loud, you probably reduced its ability to disturb you—not permanently, of course, but the repetition produced a temporary change in your emotional response to the worry.

(If you didn't get this result, review the worry you chose to make sure it's representative of your chronic worries, and replace it if it's not. If it's a representative statement, you might be dealing with a different kind of problem—depressive memories of a past event, rather than worrisome thoughts of a possible future event, for instance; or a strong obsessive-compulsive tendency. If this is the case, perhaps you should review your situation with a professional therapist skilled in this type of work.)

35: TAKE YOUR WORRIES FOR A WALK

What to Know

If you have dogs, you generally need to take those dogs for a walk, unless you have room to let them run. There will be times when you don't feel like it—when it's cold and snowy outside, when you're too busy writing a book, or when you have a headache, and you just don't feel like doing it. And then when you take those dogs for a walk, they don't always do what you want. Sometimes they race ahead, trying to pull you along. Sometimes they lag behind, and you have to make them follow. Sometimes they try to eat stuff they shouldn't, or bark at your neighbors.

But if you don't let those dogs poop and pee outdoors, pretty soon they'll do it indoors. That won't do much for your headache or your book!

Those dogs are a lot like your worrisome thoughts. Sometimes they demand attention when you really don't feel like giving it, and sometimes they just don't do things the way you wish they would. But life is better with the walks than without them!

What to Do

You've probably noticed that you tend to worry less when you're busy and more when you're idle. Episodes of chronic worry often fade faster when you're active. So, it will be useful to return your attention and energy back to involvement with the external world around you. This doesn't mean to simply make yourself busy. That's too much like trying to get rid of the thoughts. Not that there's anything terribly wrong with that, getting rid of the thoughts, if it can be done simply and effectively. It's just that trying directly to get rid of the thoughts usually makes them more persistent and plentiful. So it is with worries. It might seem like there would be a better time to go to a dinner party, but life is a come-as-you-are party, and if you're worried the night of the party, then pack up your worries and bring them with you. Would you be happier without the worries? Yes, but that choice isn't immediately available. Would you be better off lying in bed, alone with your worries? Probably not!

Go on about your business—the worries may leave sooner that way. If they don't, at least you're participating in life while you wait for them to pass. People often object to the idea of getting involved with a project of any kind, on the grounds that they will be able to do a better job when they're not worried so much. Similarly, they often want to isolate themselves from others, out of a concern that others will notice their distress and be bothered by it.

Both are instances of how our gut instincts for how to handle worry tend to be the opposite of what would actually be helpful. Both suggest that we need, first, to get rid of the worrisome thoughts we're experiencing, and then, afterward, to get involved with activities outside our skin. It's more often the other way around. Your involvement with your external world will tend to direct your energy and attention there—and leave less of it "in your head." Moreover, when you interact with the external world, you get more involved with realistic rules of thumb. When you're in your head, by contrast, you can imagine anything. This is why anticipatory worry is almost always worse than anything that actually happens in real life—in your head, anything seems possible! In the external world, the rules of reality apply.

36: WATCH YOURSELF WORRY

What to Know

Watching yourself worry sounds, on the surface, like a bizarre, unwelcome exercise. But most worry is subliminal. It occurs when we're multitasking. We worry while driving, attending lectures, showering, eating, watching television, or doing some routine work that doesn't demand much attention. And since we rarely give worry our full attention, it's easy for it to continue endlessly. Because worry comes in the form of our own subliminal thoughts, it has more power to influence us. And we all tend to assume that *if it's my thought, there must be something to it*. We tend not to notice that we can think all kinds of nonsense, that thoughts are often only anxiety symptoms, nothing more.

When you worry out loud, you don't just say the worries, you hear them. When you worry in front of a mirror, you see yourself doing the worrying. You're not just worrying in the back of your mind. You're hearing, and watching, yourself as you worry. The worry is no longer subliminal, and this will probably help you get a better perspective on it.

What to Do

Worry out loud, in front of a mirror. This will probably seem strange and awkward at first. However, if you're reading this book, you'll likely have lots of experience with worrying.

Schedule times to watch yourself worry in advance, two a day, and write them into your schedule. Pick times when you have privacy and don't have to answer the phone or the doorbell, talk to others, look after the dog or the kids, and so on. It's usually best to avoid the following times: first thing in the morning upon waking, last thing at night, or right after meals.

The advantage of doing the worrying this way is that it helps you be a better *observer* of your worry.

PART 7

MORE TOOLS FOR THE TOOLKIT

37: CHANGE YOUR INTERPRETATIONS

What to Know

Recognizing that your interpretation of a situation, rather than the situation itself, is causing anxiety gives you a new way to reduce your anxiety. You can change these interpretations to reduce amygdala activation.

Let's say that Liz is experiencing anxiety about writing assignments in her English class. Three elements are at play here: the event, the interpretation provided by Liz's cortex, and her emotion (anxiety). When Liz got a recent writing assignment back, she saw that her teacher had written many comments on the paper. She thought to herself, *All of those comments are pointing out my mistakes. I'm obviously a terrible writer, and I'm going to fail this course.* Immediately after having these thoughts, Liz felt nauseous, started trembling, and felt overwhelmed. Her thoughts had definitely activated her amygdala.

But later, when Liz actually looked at her teacher's comments, she saw that while some of them were indeed corrections, others were compliments, helpful feedback, or her teacher's reactions to thought-provoking things she had written. Her grade was a B—not a disaster, but allowing room for improvement. Now Liz has an opportunity to change her interpretation. Next time she gets a paper back with comments written on it, she can think, *My teacher is giving me helpful feedback. I'm going to learn how to be a better writer and I can get a better grade.* Clearly, these interpretations of the same event won't create the same level of anxiety.

The situations in which you feel anxiety can provide opportunities for you to examine the interpretations your cortex is providing. Keep the three elements in mind: event, interpretation, and resulting emotion. Learn to recognize your interpretations, and then consider how to modify them to reduce anxiety.

What to Do

On a separate piece of paper, list several situations in which you feel anxiety. Then, for each, see if you can identify the interpretations that lead you to react in an anxious manner.

Next, spend some time brainstorming alternative interpretations for each anxiety-igniting interpretation you identified. If you play with this a bit, you can probably see how different interpretations could lead to a wide range of emotional responses. Of course, for the purposes of reducing anxiety, you'd want to focus on interpretations that lead to a more calm, balanced state of mind. (If you need help coming up with alternative interpretations, the section on coping thoughts in chapter 28 will be helpful.)

Once you've identified alternative interpretations, try saying them out loud in order to establish them more fully. This will strengthen your ability to modify your interpretation. In the beginning, the process of changing interpretations may feel awkward; you may not find your new interpretations convincing. But with time, you'll find that these thoughts become stronger and arise on their own more often. The more you deliberately use them, the more they'll become a part of your habitual way of responding.

Changing your thoughts isn't easy, but if you devote some attention to noticing your interpretations and are dedicated to looking at situations differently, you can do it. It's worth the effort, since changing your thoughts before your amygdala is activated is much easier than calming yourself down once your amygdala gets involved.

38: REPLACE THE THOUGHT

What to Know

When people work on changing thoughts, they often complain that they can't get rid of their negative thoughts. This is a common problem that springs from how the mind works. Studies have shown that trying to erase or silence a thought simply isn't an effective approach (Wegner et al. 1987).

For example, if you're asked to not think about pink elephants, the image of pink elephants will, of course, leap into your mind, even if you haven't been thinking about pink elephants all day. And the harder you try to stop thinking about pink elephants, the more you think of them. If you have a tendency toward obsession, you're probably familiar with this pattern. Erasing a thought by constantly reminding yourself not to think about it (and therefore thinking about it) activates the circuitry storing that thought and makes it stronger.

Some people have a strong tendency to use their brain in ways that create anxiety. They are often quite talented at imagining dreadful events or coming up with negative scenarios. In fact, people who are highly creative and imaginative are sometimes more prone to anxiety for this very reason. The way they think about their life and imagine events frequently captures the attention of the amygdala and provokes a reaction. People who catastrophize or use imagery in ways that frighten them are typical examples. If this is an issue for you, think of your cortex as cable television. Despite having hundreds of channels to choose from, you get stuck on the Anxiety Channel. Unfortunately, it appears to be your favorite. You may focus on thoughts and images that have anxiety-igniting potential without realizing it. Or perhaps you're aware of this focus but argue with the thoughts, just as you might argue with televised political commentators you don't agree with. Arguing with your thoughts is similar. You don't want to spend too much time arguing with your thoughts because that tends to keep the focus on them and maintain the circuitry underlying them.

Consider Rachel, who recently had a job interview. At the time, she felt the interview went fairly well; but afterward she started rethinking some of her statements and wondering how they sounded to the person who interviewed her. Now, with each passing day Rachel feels increasingly worried about whether she'll get the position. She becomes discouraged and starts to worry she won't get the job. She begins to second-guess how she responded in the interview, becomes pessimistic, and starts to believe she won't get the job.

Rachel is definitely watching the Anxiety Channel. Notice that the interview isn't Rachel's real problem. She doesn't even know how the interview affected her chances of being hired. The Anxiety Channel is the problem. If Rachel recognizes this and, instead of focusing on worrying about the interview, begins to look at other job possibilities and prepare herself for new interviews, she'll be much more productive. If she imagines future interviews going better because of what she learned from this interview, her attitude will be much more positive. As Rachel begins to think about strategies for upcoming interviews, she finds she's no longer stuck on the Anxiety Channel.

What to Do

You might be successful in interrupting a thought by specifically telling yourself, *Stop!* This technique is called *thought stopping*. However, the next step is crucial. If you *replace* the thought with another thought, it's more likely that you'll keep the first thought out of your mind. Let's say you're working in your garden and keep worrying that at any moment you'll encounter a snake. Tell yourself, *Stop!* and then begin thinking about something else: a song on the radio, the names of the flowers you intend to plant in your garden, ideas you have for a loved one's birthday present—basically anything captivating and, ideally, pleasant. By replacing the anxiety-provoking thought with something else that engages your mind, you make it more likely that you won't return to that thought.

Therefore, "Don't erase—replace!" is the best approach with anxiety-igniting thoughts. If you notice that you're thinking something like *I can't handle this*, focus on replacing that thought with a coping thought, such as *This isn't easy, but I will get through it.* By repeating this coping thought to yourself, you'll strengthen a more adaptive way of thinking and activate circuitry that will protect you from anxiety. It takes some practice, but your new thoughts will eventually become habitual.

39: ASSESS YOUR COGNITIVE FUSION

What to Know

You can gain a great deal of cortex-based control over your anxiety if you recognize the difference between thoughts about events and the events themselves. *Cognitive fusion* occurs when we get so caught up in our thoughts that we forget they are merely thoughts. In essence, we become "fused" with our thoughts to the point that they hinder us from living our best life.

Consider Sonia, a young mother with a baby boy. One day she had a thought about how vulnerable her baby was and how easily she could harm him. Then her mind seemed to fill up with thoughts and images of different ways that she could intentionally or unintentionally hurt her baby. She imagined herself accidentally dropping him and thought about how easily she could drown him. These thoughts and images terrified her, and before long she was afraid to be alone with her son because she believed that having those awful thoughts meant she might act on them. In this way, she confused her thoughts with reality and fell victim to cognitive fusion.

Yet the very fact that she was afraid to be alone with her son demonstrated that she was concerned about his being harmed and would take action to protect him if it was necessary.

At any given time, we each have a variety of thoughts created by the cortex, but this doesn't mean that the thoughts are true, that whatever we're thinking about is going to happen, or that we're going to act on our thoughts. Still, it's all too easy to forget that thoughts are just thoughts: neural events in the cortex that may have no relationship to reality. Recognizing the difference between thoughts and actual events is essential in managing cortex-based anxiety.

What to Do

If you have a tendency to take your thoughts and feelings at face value and believe them, this habit is likely to interfere with your ability to rewire your cortex to help you resist anxiety. The cortex has a great deal of flexibility, but you have to be willing to take advantage of it. To assess your tendencies toward cognitive fusion, take a moment to read through the statements below and check any that apply to you:

☐ *If I don't worry, I'm afraid things will get worse.*

☐ *When a thought occurs to me, I find I need to take it seriously.*

☐ *Anxiety is usually a clear sign that something is about to go wrong.*

☐ *Worrying about something can sometimes prevent bad things from happening.*

☐ *When I feel ill, I need to focus on it and evaluate it.*

☐ *I'm afraid of some of my thoughts.*

☐ *When someone suggests a different way to see things, I have a hard time taking it seriously.*

☐ *If I have doubts, there are usually good reasons for them.*

☐ *The negative things I think about myself are probably true.*

☐ *When I expect to do poorly, it usually means I will do poorly.*

If you checked many of these statements, you're probably overly fused with your thoughts and feelings. You'll benefit from recognizing that just thinking or feeling something doesn't make it so. When you believe a thought represents some kind of truth, you'll have more resistance to letting go of that thought, and this can prevent you from rewiring your cortex.

40: DISCOVER COGNITIVE DEFUSION

What to Know

Cognitive fusion is quite common. We all tend to assume that what we think is reality, and don't often question our assumptions and interpretations. But sometimes people need to question their perspectives, especially in regard to distressing situations. Knowing that our assumptions are fallible is an important recognition. Cognitive fusion can generate a great deal of unnecessary anxiety.

Cognitive fusion makes people more likely to respond to the *thought* of an event in the same way they'd react if the event actually occurred. Consider Arrianna, who had trouble contacting her boyfriend one afternoon and began to worry that something bad had happened to him. She had images of his being in an accident and also thoughts that he was contemplating breaking up with her. As she considered these possibilities, she became very upset. Later, Arrianna found out that her boyfriend had left his cell phone at home and hadn't received her messages. This was a huge relief to her.

What's interesting in this story is that Arrianna reacted to the thoughts she was having as if they were actual events, and those thoughts made her anxious. Do you ever catch yourself doing something similar?

When certain anxiety-igniting thoughts are combined with cognitive fusion, the risk of creating anxiety becomes greater. If you have a tendency to have pessimistic thoughts or to worry, you'll benefit from resisting cognitive fusion. For instance, if you tend to be a pessimistic thinker, it can be helpful to remind yourself that your thoughts don't determine what happens.

Because the amygdala responds to thoughts just as it does to actual events, you may be able to greatly reduce your anxiety by being aware of anxiety-igniting thoughts and reducing the time you spend contemplating such thoughts. Although this sounds logical, surprising numbers of people worry that they must take every thought or feeling they have seriously, and some even argue that the mere existence of a thought suggests it's true, as these examples show:

- An insecure woman insisted that the fact that she didn't have confidence in herself was proof that she shouldn't have confidence in herself.

- An 85-year-old man reported that his fear of falling meant he couldn't leave his home.

- A woman was critical of her work performance and worried that she would be fired—despite never having received a bad evaluation at work.

The cortex is a busy, noisy place, often full of ideas and feelings that have no basis in reality. The problem isn't the ideas and feelings themselves, but a tendency to take them seriously. Psychologist Steven Hayes (2004, 17) has suggested that "it is the tendency to take these experiences literally and then to fight against them that is…most harmful" and offers cognitive defusion as the solution.

Cognitive defusion involves taking a different stance toward your thoughts: being aware of them without getting caught up in them.

What to Do

Examine your own anxiety experiences for evidence of cognitive fusion—accepting thoughts or feelings as true even though there's no evidence, or only weak evidence, to support them. A common example is believing a situation is dangerous because of a *feeling* that it's dangerous, rather than having actual evidence of a threat. Take some time now to make a list of examples of situations where you may be engaging in cognitive fusion. Here are some examples to get you going:

- *I think my neighbors criticize my lawn.*

- *Nobody at this party likes me.*

- *I absolutely cannot bear to have another panic attack.*

Once you've compiled your list, review it and consider how a belief in these unfounded thoughts may be contributing to your anxiety.

Cognitive defusion is a very powerful cognitive restructuring technique. Developing your ability to relate to your thoughts in this way involves not allowing yourself to take thoughts at face value and instead simply recognizing them as experiences you're having. For instance, you could acknowledge a thought without buying into it by saying, *Hmm…interesting. Once again I see that I'm having the thought that I'm never going to get my diploma.* To be successful at cognitive defusion, you need to develop a sense of yourself that doesn't get lost in the thought need processes of your cortex. You're an observer of your cortex, not a believer of everything it produces. To help distance yourself from a thought, you could tell yourself something like *I to be careful of this pesky thought. I have no reason to put faith in it, and it's likely to activate my amygdala.*

Mindfulness techniques are also very helpful, as they help you build strength and skill in focusing your thoughts on what you choose and resisting the urge to get lost in thoughts that may or may not reflect reality.

41: DEALING WITH CATASTROPHIC THINKING

What to Know

Albert Ellis was an influential 20th-century psychologist who contributed to the movement of cognitive behavioral approaches to psychotherapy. Ellis (2000) used the term *catastrophizing* to describe a human tendency to blow situations out of proportion or to turn minor threats into calamities: an increase in your heart rate means that you're having a heart attack; not being able to get a song out of your head means you're going crazy. Ellis found this thinking common among people who suffer from persistent anxieties.

Have you ever wondered why you might catastrophize? Did you observe a family member's blowing things out of proportion? Did you pick it up from watching movies? These may be contributing factors. But here's another. If you startle easily, you may be prone to catastrophize and have difficulty disengaging from negative thinking (McMillan et al. 2012). Although you cannot change a tendency to startle easily, you can teach yourself to disengage from negative thinking.

Catastrophizing goes hand in hand with *awfulizing*, which means turning a bad situation into something worse (Ellis and Harper 1997). You might use alarmist language, such as "awful" or "terrible," to describe events. In this case, your inner message is that what you're feeling is worse than bad. Think again. Awfulizing amplifies what you don't like. On the other hand, toning down your language might do you considerable good. For example, substitute "unpleasant" for "awful" and see if this makes a difference.

What to Do

In a catastrophic state of mind, you're likely to focus on what's troubling you and to neglect examining your thinking. If you find yourself catastrophizing, a solution is to think about your thinking.

Since catastrophizing is adding surplus negative meaning to a situation, you can tone down your thinking by deleting the added meaning. A good way to do this is to start with a general statement about the current effects of your anxiety and then to ask yourself what will happen next. This "and then what?" approach will help deflate a catastrophic thinking process.

Suppose you don't pass an important test. You might tell yourself that your life is ruined. You might imagine that people who know of this failure will run from you as if you had a contagious disease. But is any of this true? Take the general statement, "My life is ruined." If this is what you say to yourself, you can question your thinking by asking, "And then what?" You might conclude, *I'll be miserable*. And then what? *I'll likely get back to my normal life*. And then what? You might conclude, *I'll study and retake the test*. If retaking the test is the bottom line, then why not go directly to that solution and bypass the catastrophic part of the process?

42: POSITIVE FOCUS

What to Know

Conventional wisdom says that we should be punished for doing wrong so that we will want to do right instead. In every situation we encounter, we tend to keep our focus on noticing what we're doing wrong. While negative reinforcement does help us learn when it comes from our environment, for instance learning not to grab a rose by the stem, it's rarely effective when it comes from other people or from ourselves. We learn best when we're consistently rewarded for what we're doing right.

This is true for learning anything new and difficult. A pianist who is praised by their teacher for their focus and expression—even when they miss notes—will ultimately make better music than an equally talented pianist who is praised only when they perform flawlessly. A basketball player who is praised by their coach for shooting with correct form—regardless of whether they hit the basket—is more likely to develop a good shot than a similar player who is praised only when their attempts are successful.

When it comes to changing your own behavior, the lesson is the same, except you're the one who has to give the praise. In your practice, you're both teacher and student, both player and coach. As teacher, you make the lesson plan. You set a conscious intention that you, the student, will practice incorporating a more positive focus and praising yourself.

What to Do

Acting as a teacher or a coach for yourself may feel awkward, but it's a role you need to be aggressive about. Sure, patting yourself on the back seems silly, but it's nowhere near as silly as kicking yourself in the butt for not being perfect. That is just plain ridiculous.

When you practice strategies to calm your intrusive thoughts, be your own coach and teacher. Praise your planning, praise your execution, praise your courage welcoming negative feelings. Praise everything about your practice except the outcome!

43: DEFUSING "HOT BUTTON" WORDS

What to Know

Do you have some "hot button" words that you prefer to avoid, to skim over if you see them in print—words you don't want to say aloud because they might lead you to feel anxious?

You probably do, if you let your mind ponder it for a few moments. People with panic attacks often want to avoid words like "faint," "cerebral hemorrhage," "screaming insanity," and so on. People with social anxiety aren't so fond of words like "sweat," "tremble," and "blush." People with intrusive obsessive thoughts tend to avoid the key words from those thoughts, like "murder," "poison," "stab," "insecticide," and so on. Even people with just basic, garden variety anxiety have words that carry some special, "fused" feeling for them.

Consider the example of a young child who gets scratched by the family cat. Young Lucia may feel afraid of that cat for a while, feel afraid of other cats and dogs, run away from a cat commercial on TV, or even burst into tears or show signs of distress at the word "cat." She can feel fear when she hears the word, even when the cat is outside. Lucia has given the word "cat" the properties of scratchiness and "biteyness" that actually belong only to the animal. As a result, she can become afraid in the absence of the cat, just from hearing the word, or maybe even thinking the word. She no longer makes a distinction between hearing the word "cat" and seeing a cat leap at her, claws outspread.

As her parents notice this, they may try to help keep Lucia calm by using some code to refer to "cat." Maybe they use pig Latin (Ixnay on the atcay!) or refer to it as a banana rather than a cat. They're trying to care for Lucia and protect her from upset. But they are also, unwittingly, strengthening the association Lucia has formed between the sound of the word "cat" and those hurtful properties of "bitey-ness" and scratchiness.

In the same way, some support groups for people with panic attacks ask members to refrain from using the word "breathing" because some members are sensitive to this word and will have trouble catching their "b" if someone uses the "b" word! The group has fused the word "breathing" with the sensations of hyperventilation and all the symptoms that accompany it. Here we see people, intending to be kind and protective, acting in ways that lead others to feel more vulnerable, rather than less, to the "b" word.

What to Do

Take one of your "hot button" words and repeat it, out loud if you have the privacy to do that—twenty-five times. This technique aims to break the link you may have established between a word or thought and the actual properties you have come to associate with that thought. You can even engage in playful exercises that use, and overuse, the word. For instance, Lucia's parents might help her to break apart the word "cat" from those properties of scratchiness and "biteyness" by making nonsense rhymes with the word cat, singing songs about cats, rhyming the word "cat," making artwork based on the word "cat," and so on. If young Lucia does that with the word "cat," the word will probably start to lose its claws.

44: DEAL WITH SOCIAL ANXIETY

What to Know

Our lives are significantly shaped by our beliefs and emotions, and so we expect ourselves to feel and act in certain ways based on the social context we are in. However, at least some of our excess painful social emotions (such as social anxiety, shame, embarrassment, self-consciousness) are associated with false expectations and beliefs. When belief-based anxieties and fears weave through your social life, you have a significant challenge to get beyond these interferences if you choose to do and feel better in social settings.

Do you have social anxieties and fears that merit correcting?

What to Do

Here are fifty ways to combat your social anxieties:

Keep fighting fear. Fear of fear feeds on itself. Plan to survive this temporary discomfort. You'll find that you can survive it. Emotional tolerance is a prelude to feeling more comfortable with yourself in social situations.

Maintain perspective. Avoid focusing on your fears. Instead, ask others questions about themselves. You'll find that people are more than happy to talk about themselves.

Watch the worry. You fret about possibly acting inept. Correct this worry by instructing yourself to suspend judgment. Then act as if you were capable of communicating well with most others.

Give up playing Nostradamus. Predicting the world will crash down on you if you make a social blunder is an imaginary crisis. The anxiety from such false predictions is real enough. But you can work on catching yourself making predictions and on shifting to more realistic thinking.

Avoid anticipatory anxiety. If you catastrophize about future dangers to your ego, picture yourself breaking a magnifying glass, and then imagine that your catastrophizing vision is shattered.

Level your language. Hyperbole, such as "I will disgrace myself forever if I make a social misstep," is an egregious over-generalization. Intentionally make a minor misstep to show yourself that it's not the end of the world.

Beware of your definitions. Define a type of social event as a staging ground for looking like a fool, and you're likely to feel the way that you think. Redefine the event in a more positive light, and you will feel better.

Accept feeling awkward. Your feelings may be factual, but they are not the same as facts. If you're anxious about being socially awkward, realize that some people will find your manner charming. Try to take an "it is as it is" acceptance view.

Handle self-handicapping. Don't avoid a social gathering with the excuse that you'll fail. Instead, imagine yourself cordially communicating.

Defeat your needless inhibitions. Practice doing something as basic as introducing yourself to people in a group.

Temper your timidity. Mingle softly rather than not at all.

Pen yourself in. Instead of waiting for someone to rescue you, push yourself to participate.

Keep it light. You don't have to make all brilliant remarks.

Bring yourself into the fold. Make a comment about something in the immediate area, such as the weather.

Address your ambivalence. Asking yourself, *Should I or should I not say something?* is a formula for letting a conversation float past you. Assume that you should, and you're likely to be right.

Think less doubtfully. Abandon second-guessing yourself about what you should say. When in doubt, speak up.

Don't let your mind go blank. You can always say hello.

Retreat from rejection. Fear of rejection is ordinarily a fictional fear. If someone justifiably rejects an idea of yours, you can still accept the parts of your idea that remain valid.

Use bashfulness as a positive signal. Instead of looking aloof, look at others as potential friends.

Manage your modesty. Get into the daily habit of sharing a positive attribute that characterizes you. You may blush less.

Watch your wariness. Don't take a back seat. Assume that some of the people whom you meet will be friendly. See if you can find them.

Accept feeling shy. If you're naturally shy, you won't eliminate this natural tendency. However, you can choose to manage your shyness. Try to discover other people's special interests by asking them questions. Do this and you may be seen as a brilliant conversationalist, even if you say little about yourself.

You don't have to be bold. Try communicating in a nonassertive, low-key way.

Don't expect immediate jubilance. If you warm to new social situations slowly, know that you are not alone and not odd.

Avoid blaming your amygdala. Social anxieties correlate with a sensitive amygdala. Nevertheless, you can buffer yourself from needless stress by habituating to it. That means practice, practice, practice communicating to others until you're no longer afraid.

Downplay listening to your heart. Attending to your heartbeat shifts your focus from what you're doing to how tense you feel. Participate. Your heart will take care of itself.

Mind your body language. Habitually gaze downward and you'll look insecure. Hold your head up. Glance around without staring. This signals confidence.

Nod your head yes. Nodding signals approval. Most people like approval.

Try to smile. Think of something pleasing and let your smile extend from the thought.

Don't read too much into facial expressions. Assumptions about the causes and meanings of others' facial expressions are risky. We do have an inborn tendency to read faces, but not all faces are easy to read.

Attend to the facts. Shift from self-absorbing thoughts to objective observation of what is going on. Respond based on an objective awareness.

Reevaluate. To avoid rejection, you believe you must make a great first impression. Plan to make a reasonable impression, and let the chips fall where they may.

Ditch your false expectations. You don't need to be the life of the party if that is not your style.

Flip things around. If you fear total rejection, instead of withering in silence in the corner, pretend that you'll get a million dollars to engage 10 percent of the time. You can do it.

Don't think you must dominate. Show interest. Share a few thoughts. Let others talk. Put in your two cents' worth when a topic appeals to you.

Prepare to be pleasantly surprised. You may make serendipitous connections with people.

Don't wait to say only perfect things. Accept the concept of the cocktail party syndrome. People will rarely stay on topic and will invariably introduce their own agendas into a discussion.

Avoid conditionals for socializing. Waiting to feel comfortable before venturing out rarely works well. It's a form of procrastinating. Test the waters and see if social comfort follows.

Quell your self-consciousness. You're probably more aware of your state of mind than anyone else is.

Separate anxiety from context. If you act socially fearful in some situations but not others, how does what you tell yourself differ in these contexts?

Challenge feeling inferior. Instead of concentrating on what you think you lack, play on the strengths that you have.

Exercise your strongest social skills. List what they are. Use one each time you're part of a social gathering.

Ditch the shame. You're not globally worthless for being you. You just think you're something that you're really not.

Derail irrational guilt. It's silly to condemn yourself for errors that only you observe.

Speak up. As you practice speaking up, it gets easier.

Don't defect-detect. For every fault you find in yourself, find a positive attribute that others may observe.

Don't be coy. Evasiveness is likely to bring negative attention.

Think ahead. Plan to live through social tensions. Eventually you'll have fewer to live through.

Resist withdrawing into a bottle of wine. Alcohol-dulled senses are a staging ground for problems and for tensions that are catalysts for further drinking.

Realize you can't win them all. Nobody is a universal crowd-pleaser.

FURTHER READING

Anxiety and Avoidance: *A Universal Treatment for Anxiety, Panic, and Fear* by Michael A. Tompkins, PhD

Anxiety Happens: *52 Ways to Find Peace of Mind* by John P. Forsyth, PhD, and Georg H. Eifert, PhD

CBT Workbook for Anxiety: *A Step-by-Step Program* by William J. Knaus, EdD

DBT Skills Workbook for Anxiety: *Breaking Free from Worry, Panic, PTSD, and Other Anxiety Symptoms* by Alexander L. Chapman, PhD, Kim L. Gratz, PhD, and Matthew T. Tull, PhD

Don't Feed the Monkey Mind: *How to Stop the Cycle of Anxiety, Fear, and Worry* by Jennifer Shannon, LMFT

How to Be Miserable: *40 Strategies You Already Use* by Randy J. Paterson, PhD

Just a Thought: *A No-Willpower Approach to Overcome Self-Doubt and Make Peace with Your Mind* by Amy Johnson, PhD

MBSR Workbook for Anxiety by Bob Stahl, PhD, Florence Meleo-Meyer, MS, MA, and Lynn Koerbel, MPH

The Mindfulness and Acceptance Workbook for Anxiety: *A guide to Breaking Free from Anxiety, Phobias, and Worry using Acceptance and Commitment Therapy* by John P. Forsyth, PhD, and Georg H. Eifert, PhD

Mindfulness Workbook for OCD: *A Guide to Overcoming Obsessions and Compulsions Using Mindfulness and Cognitive Behavioral Therapy* by Jon Hershfield, MFT, and Tom Corboy, MFT

Needing to Know for Sure: *A CBT-Based Guide to Overcoming Compulsive Checking and Reassurance Seeking* by Martin M. Seif, PhD, and Sally M. Winston, PsyD

Overcoming Anticipatory Anxiety: *A CBT Guide for Moving past Chronic Indecisiveness, Avoidance, and Catastrophic Thinking* by Sally M. Winston, PsyD, and Martin N. Seif, PhD

Overcoming Unwanted Intrusive Thoughts: *A CBT-Based Guide to Getting Over Frightening, Obsessive, or Disturbing Thoughts* by Sally M. Winston, PsyD, and Marin N. Seif, PhD

Rewire Your Anxious Brain: *How to Use the Neuroscience of Fear to End Anxiety, Panic, and Worry* by Catherine M. Pittman, PhD, and Elizabeth M. Karle, MLIS

What Happened to Make You Anxious: *How to Uncover the Little 't' Traumas that Drive Your Anxiety, Worry, and Fear* by Jamie Castillo, LCSW

The Worry Trick: *How Your Brain Tricks You into Expecting the Worst and What You Can Do About It* by David A. Carbonell, PhD

REFERENCES

Einstein, D. A., and R. G. Menzies. 2004. "Role of Magical Thinking in Obsessive-Compulsive Symptoms in an Undergraduate Sample." *Depression and Anxiety* 19 (3): 174–79.

Ellis, A. 2000. *How to Control Your Anxiety Before It Controls You*. New York: Citadel Press.

Ellis, A., and R. A. Harper. 1997. *A Guide to Rational Living*. 3rd ed. North Hollywood, CA: Wilshire Book Company.

Hayes, S. C. 2004. "Acceptance and Commitment Therapy and the New Behavior Therapies." In *Mindfulness and Acceptance: Expanding the Cognitive-Behavioral Tradition*, edited by S. C. Hayes, V. M. Follette, and M. M. Linehan. New York: Guilford.

Hayes, S. C., with S. Smith. 2005. *Get Out of Your Mind and Into Your Life: The New Acceptance and Commitment Therapy*. Oakland, CA: New Harbinger Publications.

McMillan, K. A., G. J. Asmundson, M. J. Zvolensky, and R. N. Carleton. 2012. "Startle Response and Anxiety Sensitivity: Subcortical Indices of Physiologic Arousal and Fear Responding." *Emotion* 12 (6): 1264–72.

Olatunji, B. O., K. Naragon-Gainey, and K. B. Wolitzky-Taylor. 2013. "Specificity of Rumination in Anxiety and Depression: A Multimodal Meta-Analysis." *Clinical Psychology: Science and Practice* 20 (3): 225–57.

Schwartz, J. M., and S. Begley. 2003. *The Mind and the Brain: Neuroplasticity and the Power of Mental Force*. New York: Harper Collins.

Wegner, D., D. Schneider, S. Carter, and T. White. 1987. "Paradoxical Effects of Thought Suppression." *Journal of Personality and Social Psychology* 53: 5–13.

Jon Hershfield, MFT, is director of The Center for OCD and Anxiety at Sheppard Pratt in Towson, MD. He specializes in the use of mindfulness and cognitive behavioral therapy (CBT) for obsessivecompulsive disorder (OCD) and related disorders. He is author of Overcoming Harm OCD, When a Family Member Has OCD, and The OCD Workbook for Teens; and coauthor of The Mindfulness Workbook for OCD and Everyday Mindfulness for OCD.

Tom Corboy, MFT, is executive director of the OCD Center of Los Angeles, which he founded in 1999. He is a licensed psychotherapist specializing in mindfulness-based cognitive behavioral therapy (MBCBT) for the treatment of OCD and related anxietybased conditions. In addition to his work with individual clients, he has trained and mentored many postgraduate interns, has presented at numerous conferences held by the International OCD Foundation (IOCDF), and has facilitated weekly therapy groups for adults with OCD since 1997.

Sally M. Winston, PsyD, is founder and codirector of the Anxiety and Stress Disorders Institute of Maryland in Towson, MD. She served as first chair of the Anxiety and Depression Association of America (ADAA) Clinical Advisory Board, and received their prestigious Jerilyn Ross Clinician Advocate Award. She is a master clinician who has given soughtafter workshops for therapists for decades. She is coauthor of What Every Therapist Needs to Know About Anxiety Disorders and Overcoming Unwanted Intrusive Thoughts.

Martin N. Seif, PhD, is cofounder of the ADAA, and was a member of its board of directors from 1977 through 1991. Seif is former associate director of the Anxiety and Phobia Treatment Center at White Plains Hospital, a faculty member of New YorkPresbyterian Hospital, and is board certified in cognitive behavioral psychology from the American

Board of Professional Psychology. He maintains a private practice in New York, NY; and Greenwich, CT; and is coauthor of What Every Therapist Needs to Know About Anxiety Disorders and Overcoming Unwanted Intrusive Thoughts.

Catherine M. Pittman, PhD, is a licensed clinical psychologist specializing in the treatment of anxiety disorders and brain injuries. She is professor of psychology at Saint Mary's College in Notre Dame, IN; where she has taught for more than thirty years.

Elizabeth M. Karle, MLIS, is collection management supervisor at the CushwaLeighton Library at Saint Mary's College in Notre Dame, IN. In addition to supplying research for this book, she has personal experience with anxiety disorders—providing a firsthand perspective that focuses the book on what is most useful for the anxiety sufferer. Originally from Illinois, she currently resides in South Bend, IN; and holds degrees or certificates from the University of Notre Dame, Roosevelt University, and Dominican University. She is author of Hosting a Library Mystery.

William J. Knaus, EdD, is a licensed psychologist with more than fortysix years of clinical experience working with people suffering from anxiety, depression, and procrastination. He has appeared on numerous regional and national television shows, including The Today Show, and more than one hundred radio shows. His ideas have appeared in national magazines such as U.S. News & World Report and Good Housekeeping, and major newspapers such as The Washington Post and the Chicago Tribune. He is one of the original directors of postdoctoral psychotherapy training in rational emotive behavior therapy (REBT). Knaus is author or coauthor of more than twentyfive books, including The Cognitive Behavioral Workbook for Depression and The Procrastination Workbook.

Jennifer Shannon, LMFT, is a psychotherapist, and author of Don't Feed the Monkey Mind, The Anxiety Survival Guide for Teens, and A Teen's Guide to Getting Stuff Done. She is a diplomate of the Academy of Cognitive Therapy.

David A. Carbonell, PhD, is a clinical psychologist who specializes in treating anxiety in all its forms. He is author of Panic Attacks Workbook, The Worry Trick, and Fear of Flying Workbook. He is "coach" on the popular selfhelp website, www.anxietycoach.com, and has taught workshops on the treatment of anxiety disorders to more than 9,000 professional psychotherapists in the US and abroad. He is a longstanding member of the ADAA, and a frequent presenter at their annual conferences. He received his doctorate in clinical psychology from DePaul University in 1985, and has maintained a practice devoted to the treatment of anxiety disorders since 1990. He lives in Chicago, IL; with his wife and a pair of rescue dogs. In his spare time, he is a founding member of The Therapy Players, an improvisational comedy troupe of professional psychotherapists which performs at clubs, theaters, and mental health conferences throughout the Chicago area.

Amy Johnson, PhD, is a coach, author, and speaker who shares a new paradigm for how our mind works that leads to lasting freedom from anxiety, depression, insecurity, and unwanted habits. She is author of Being Human, The Little Book of Big Change, and Just a Thought, and has been a regularly featured expert on The Steve Harvey Show and in The Wall Street Journal.

Real change *is* possible

For more than forty-five years, New Harbinger has published proven-effective self-help books and pioneering workbooks to help readers of all ages and backgrounds improve mental health and well-being, and achieve lasting personal growth. In addition, our spirituality books offer profound guidance for deepening awareness and cultivating healing, self-discovery, and fulfillment.

Founded by psychologist Matthew McKay and Patrick Fanning, New Harbinger is proud to be an independent, employee-owned company. Our books reflect our core values of integrity, innovation, commitment, sustainability, compassion, and trust. Written by leaders in the field and recommended by therapists worldwide, New Harbinger books are practical, accessible, and provide real tools for real change.

newharbingerpublications

MORE BOOKS from
NEW HARBINGER PUBLICATIONS